Making Holidays Special

Céleste perrino Walker

D1636758

Making Holidays Special

Céleste perrino Walker

PACIFIC PRESS® PUBLISHING ASSOCIATION
Nampa, Idaho
Oshawa, Ontario, Canada
www.PacificPress.com

Designed by Michelle C. Petz
Cover photo by John Baker and Getty Images

Additional copies of this book are available by calling toll free
1-800-765-6955 or visiting AdventistBookCenter.com

Scripture quotations marked NKJV are from the *Holy Bible,* New King James Version,
copyright © 1979, 1980, 1982 by Thomas Nelson, Inc. Used by permission.

Library of Congress Cataloging-in-Publication data

Walker, Celeste Perrino
Making holidays special : simple traditions to strengthen family ties and
deepen spiritual connections / Céleste perrino Walker
p. cm.
ISBN: 0-8163-1956-1
1. Holidays—United States. 2. Family—Religious life.
3. Seventh-day Adventists—Doctrines. I. Title.
GT4803.A2 W35 2003
394.26—dc21   2002035500

03 04 05 06 07 • 5 4 3 2 1

This book is dedicated to my paternal grandmother,

Pauline LaVigne Perrino,

for all the wonderful holidays I spent on 21 Florida Avenue in Winooski.

You made entertaining look so effortless.

Acknowledgments

I would like to thank all the wonderful, people who answered my "CALLING ALL ADVENTISTS" emails and took the time to forward them on to friends. I enjoyed corresponding with you. It is thanks to everyone who cared enough to share traditions with me that you are holding this book in your hands. I pray that God will bless each of you richly in your traditions and in your daily lives.

Contents

Preface

I believe that celebrations are an important part of our lives and experiences. It is in these mountaintop times that we forge bonds with God and each other that are hard for Satan to break. As I wrote *Making Sabbath Special* and *Adventist Family Traditions* I realized what a valuable resource our shared traditions are. They are gifts of joy we can offer each other.

Your positive response to these books has convinced me that Adventists are looking for creative ways to celebrate, whether the occasion is sacred or secular. I believe we all want ways to make our celebrations more meaningful and unique. As I write this, the Christmas holiday season is in full swing and I can't help but be grateful for all the wonderful traditions that surround not only this winter season, but every season throughout the year. Holidays give us many opportunities to celebrate our relationships and our Creator.

When I asked you to send me your holiday traditions the response was overwhelming! One great blessing in being part of such a large church family is that we can all share and learn from each other. My own family's traditions changed and grew as I gathered material for *Making Sabbath Special, Adventist Family Traditions,* and *Making Holidays Special* The traditions you sent blessed us and enriched our own circle of traditions. And I am confident that you will be blessed as we share these new traditions that form our holidays and our holy days.

Holiday traditions are the moments that define our seasons. When I asked for your holiday traditions I wondered what I might discover, what sort of trends I might expect. Based on my overview from *Adventist Family Traditions*, I expected that family would rank high in your traditions, and it did. Anniversaries and birthdays are important to you. Religious holidays had many traditions as well. But, no matter what the holiday, family is the priority. Adventists are family oriented. We are also service oriented. And we like to cook. Many of you sent me wonderful recipes. At great personal cost I "tested" several (and in some cases re-tested and re-tested). I believe they will make delicious additions to your holiday table.

It was a treat to spend time with you and learn what made your holidays special. As I cut and pasted your traditions, stories and recipes into the text of this book it reminded me of a giant scrapbook. I pictured all of us sitting around a large table, in a cozy kitchen, perhaps with a fire in a nearby fireplace and tea steaming in mugs beside us. And someone baked cookies! Spread out on the table before us are photos and recipe cards and greeting cards. As we laugh and reminisce, we fill up the pages of a big scrapbook on the table, creating this collection of Adventist holiday traditions. I hope you enjoy the many traditions shared from the hearts and homes of Adventists everywhere.

The difference between a tradition and something you "just do" is the meaning it has in your life. I hope you'll find that many of the traditions included in this book bring new meaning to your holidays. And I'd like to thank everyone who contributed traditions for sharing the joy of your holidays with us.

Céleste perrino Walker
Wyndwith
December 3, 2001

CHAPTER ONE

New Year's and Epiphany

It seemed only logical to start our traditions at the beginning of the year. New Year's is one of those holiday traditions I have always liked. I probably started celebrating New Year's when I was about fifteen or sixteen, mostly because I was always babysitting that night and had to be up anyway. I began the custom of writing out my New Year's resolutions. There were a couple of rules. First, they had to be written down *before* the ball dropped in Times Square (which I have always considered the official beginning of each new year). Second, they had to improve upon the previous year's resolutions, which meant I had to check back on how I'd done the year before in keeping my resolutions. Sometimes that was educational, other times it was more embarrassing than anything.

Over the years I even developed categories of resolutions. I had personal ones, spiritual ones, and physical ones. I still write my resolutions before the ball drops, but it's easier now. My new resolution encompasses every area of my life and takes only moments to write. Simplify. My goal is to simplify each area of my life so that I can enjoy it to the fullest. Sometimes I embellish that a bit, but the essence stays the same.

NEW YEAR'S RESOLUTIONS

Here's a little worksheet in case you'd like to try my tradition of making resolutions. Remember to check back next year and see how you did!

PERSONAL RESOLUTIONS:
1.
2.
3.

SPIRITUAL RESOLUTIONS:
1.
2.
3.

PHYSICAL RESOLUTIONS:
1.
2.
3.

I wouldn't mind spending New Year's with my young friend Petrine Knight. Sounds like she has a blast. "New Year's there's usually an all night service at the church (if New Year's falls on a Sabbath). The cousins and my sis and I camp out in the attic of my aunt's house in Brooklyn, New York. We watch all the New Year's specials and wait for the ball to drop in Times Square. That's a special thing cuz we do it every year."

During some seasons I would have to say I believe holiday traditions are positively essential for our mental health. That has to be true of New Year's. Following Christmas as closely as it does, it helps to alleviate some of the "let down" you feel after the big day. New Year's is also a traditional party evening. My husband's family used to have big New Year's Eve parties. We played all manner of games, with Rook, Up and Down, and Balderdash being the favorites. There were plenty of munchies and the traditional toast of sparkling cider at midnight.

RACHEL KINNE'S ALABAMA "CAVIAR" DIP

Rachel says, "This is a good dip to use on New Year's Eve or New Year's Day. Southern tradition says that if you eat black-eyed peas on New Year's it will bring money your way."

2 cans black-eyed peas, drained
½ cup chopped onions
½ cup chopped bell pepper
1 jalapeño chili pepper, seeded and chopped
1 clove garlic, chopped
1 tablespoon minced fresh parsley
¼ cup sugar
¼ cup red wine vinegar
1 teaspoon salt
Black pepper, to taste
Tabasco sauce, to taste

Mix vegetables. Dissolve sugar, vinegar, and salt over heat. Cool and pour over vegetables. Refrigerate 12 hours. Add black pepper and Tabasco sauce to taste. Serve with corn chips or tortilla chips.

These days we celebrate quieter. Rob and I usually stay up and have a toast, but it's been quite a while since we went to a New Year's party. The Jay Thomas family also has a quiet celebration. "New Year's we celebrate at sundown (the biblical beginning of each new day) and praise God for choosing such a logical and convenient time for the date change, giving us a chance to get to bed on time."

Mary Allen told me about a New Year's tradition that, being a Yankee, I had never heard of. "We have a New Year's Day tradition," she told me. "Being from the deep South my husband's family always celebrated New Year's Day with black-eyed peas and cornbread. They said the number of peas you ate meant how many wonderful blessings you would receive. We have perpetuated this tradition and each New Year's we have all the folks we can pack in to share it with. It is a nice break from all the rich fare of the prior holidays and so everyone is relaxed and happy. We often share memories of this day."

By and large, I didn't receive many New Year's traditions. Personally, I think it's a great holiday to celebrate. Christianity is all about fresh starts, being thankful for God's past watchcare and looking forward to what He has in store for you in the future. New Year's gives us the opportunity to celebrate all that. Maybe this year will be the one you start a New Year's tradition.

EPIPHANY

Epiphany or Festival of the Three Kings or Twelfth Day, whatever you choose to call it, is a nice little celebration following Christmas that keeps the spirit of the holiday alive. There are many aspects of the celebration that I like, but the most important is that unlike Christmas, you aren't fighting any commercial marketing extravaganza. The entire holiday is focused solely on Christ.

Epiphany always falls on the 6th of January. There's a lot to the history of it and it's worth looking up if you are interested, but for our purposes it's enough to say that it's a celebration of when the Magi found the Baby Jesus. It signifies the end of the Christmas season. Every year we've done a little more for Epiphany. This year I think we arrived at what our holiday will consist of. It was very special.

Practically speaking the requirements of Epiphany are relatively simple. First, you need a cake. This is called a Three Kings Cake. There are many variations on this. I made a type of traditional French Kings Cake, which is like a croissant filled with almond paste. Between the layers (or in the batter) of the cake you hide three féves (beans). These represent the three wise men. When I was young my mother used coins until she decided money was too dirty to put in a cake. The tradition actually began with coins in the fourteenth century when the cake was used as a type of lottery to choose a leader. Over the years the coin was substituted with a bean. Now, in some places, féves have evolved into collectible items. I'm still using beans.

When I was growing up we were told that whoever had a féve in their cake would get to make a wish for the new year. It's just fun to see if your piece of cake has one whether you wish or not. If you have a féve you are one of the honorary "wise men."

This year I took inspiration from Tasha Tudor and made a Nativity scene (OK, so far it's just Baby Jesus in a basket, but I'm working on a large crèche). I placed it a distance from the house, beneath some overhanging brush in the meadow. As I walked back I "planted" tapers in the snow and lit them so that when I reached home and looked back the way I had come the path to my Nativity scene was lit. It was snowing this year and the scene was beautiful. I could even hear the snow hiss as it hit a taper occasionally, but none of them went out.

My family gathered then and "set out" to find Baby Jesus. As we followed the path of candles we sang Christmas carols. I have to tell you the children were so excited it was hard to keep them from running ahead. When we "found" the Baby Jesus we sang a few more carols and then headed back to the house. Though I had set the table formally, the meal was simple, after which we had the cake.

Each of the children received a small present as well, something held back from Christmas, to represent the gifts of the Magi. It doesn't have to be anything expensive. Before or after dinner it's nice to read the story of the Magi and how they searched for Jesus. And you could get real ambitious and play games after the meal as well. My mother-in-law, Nancy, remembers when she was a child how they would save the Christmas tree to be burned on Epiphany. Eventually I'd like to include this practice (if local fire ordinances allow it) as well as inviting guests to celebrate with us.

Maybe this is a tradition you'd like to add to your calendar. I think that one of the reasons it is so special to me is because it's "mine," it's one I've adopted. We celebrate Christmas and most other major holidays away from home, but Epiphany is celebrated close to the family hearth and there's something soothing in that, as though as a family we have stepped back from the bustle of Christmas to really give tribute to the One it's all about.

CHAPTER TWO

Valentine's Day

I have to confess I have a soft spot for Valentine's Day, as it happens to be my wedding anniversary. Because of this the holiday has taken on a much greater significance than simply Valentine's Day alone. But, our anniversary tends to overshadow the actual holiday. Valentine's feels like it *belongs* to us, personally.

We don't have any terribly creative ways of celebrating. The children receive a present, usually a book, and a small amount of candy. There's so much candy floating around on this holiday that it has never made sense to contribute to it much ourselves. Rob's grandmother always makes us an anniversary cake and we receive lots of chocolates. Rob usually takes me out to dinner.

Now that we homeschool, the children like to pass out valentines to their friends. We try to stay away from commercial movie-type characters, and make an exception only for VeggieTales or winsome characters like Winnie the Pooh. Last year the children decorated shoebox "mailboxes" at our homeschool co-op day and then passed out their valentines, filling everyone's boxes. It was a big hit and sure to be repeated this year.

Pamela Ahlfeld, Associate Professor of Nursing at Southern Adventist University, began a Valentine's Day tradition with her family that became even more popular than she dreamed it would. "My children are now adults (20 and 23) living at home and attending SAU and though they probably wouldn't admit it, they still expect this on Valentine's Day.

"It's a tradition I started when they were in elementary school. Since my husband usually got home late from work and we all had our various activities in the latter part of the day, I started having a special Valentine's breakfast each year. We have a bigger breakfast than the usual cereal/milk or bagel—such as French toast, eggs and Prosage or Stripples, juice, etc. There are Valentine's decorations, of course—plates, cups, napkins, a special centerpiece for the table, and a small gift for each person.

"A couple of years ago I was away the week of Valentine's Day, and told them I had left items for the breakfast (the decorations, gifts, and Rice Krispies Valentine cereal). I wondered if they would even bother with it (except for the gifts, of course). I was pleased to learn that they had the special time even without me."

"Our church had an Iranian vegetarian dinner catered to our fellowship hall. We also had a program about Iran put on by an Iranian University student with Crossroads International. It was well attended."
ARDIE EARHART

No matter how elaborately or simply you celebrate, Valentine's

Day is a wonderful opportunity to tell others how much they mean to you. Sadly, that's something we often overlook on a daily basis and it can mean so much. I remember as a teenager hoping to get a carnation on Valentine's Day. At our school you put in your "order" for carnations and they were delivered. Sometimes there was a message identifying the sender; sometimes it was anonymous. It was always a matter of supreme excitement to see if you'd be one of the lucky ones to receive a carnation. I don't believe I ever received one.

You can probably think of one awkward teen who would love to get flowers this Valentine's Day. Just think of the difference you could make by saying you care. Why not start a new tradition of your own?

CHAPTER THREE

Easter

Easter is one of those holidays I never gave much deep, serious thought to until I became a parent. I just took it for granted that Easter meant celebrating the Resurrection and spending time with family. Raising children forces you to rethink what you believe and how you celebrate. Having grown up a Catholic, I have memories of spending Good Friday afternoon in silence during the hours Jesus was on the cross. This made a big impression on me at the time. It was a pretty solemn day. My own family doesn't do this any more, but I don't think it's such a bad idea to spend those hours contemplating what Jesus went through for us and might incorporate this into our holiday traditions at some point.

On Sunday morning we hunted for our Easter baskets and went to mass. After mass my grandmother made a big Easter dinner. We always had nice new dresses, this was during the years when even little girls had hats and purses to match, and we wore little gloves. Easter was a "dressy" occasion.

The first thing to hit you about Easter after becoming a parent is, of course, the Easter Bunny. We don't "do" Santa, so it seemed only logical to forego the Easter Bunny as well. The second big decision is what to put in the Easter Basket. Candy abounds at Easter. You'd think it sprang from the ground along with the crocuses and daffodils. It's hard to teach health as you hand your youngsters a basket stuffed with candy. But, when you're young, the candy is part of the fun. We subscribe to the quality over quantity theory and compromise by giving a few pieces of high quality candy, rather than bags full of waxy, commercial stuff. If you're going to eat candy, you might as well eat the good stuff.

There are a few presents included too. This part of our tradition is from Rob's side of the family. When he was growing up his Easter baskets were filled with presents rather than candy because his sister was diabetic. We keep the presents fun, but useful. This year, for instance, Joshua received a Venus flytrap (because he's plant/animal crazy) and Rachel received a rocking chair for her favorite doll (she's normally a tomboy, so this is a huge deal).

In our area there are no special Adventist Easter services on Easter Sunday. I think it would be nice to have them. The children look for their baskets, which Rob or I hide outside if the weather is nice, inside if it's not. We have a nice breakfast with croissants or homemade cinnamon rolls on the menu. Then we head up to my parent's house for Easter dinner. This consists of a two-hour drive both ways, so it pretty much takes the rest of the day.

Our Easter traditions leave a lot to be desired. I think we have the skeleton of the house and could stand to build on it. That's why I was so thrilled with some of the Easter traditions you sent me. Lora Hendrickson even mentioned the Easter Story Cookies, which I have the recipe for but had forgotten about. It gave us a good excuse to try them out.

"Each ingredient/event in making the Easter Cookies also has a spiritual message (vinegar, beating the nuts, etc.). Then we make the Easter Cookies recipe that you seal in the oven for the night. The cookies are empty the next morning, just like Jesus' tomb was Easter morning."

EASTER STORY COOKIE RECIPE
Author unknown

You will need:

1 cup whole pecans	Wooden spoon
3 egg whites	Zipper baggie
1 cup sugar	Tape
1 tsp. vinegar	Bible
Pinch salt	

1. Preheat oven to 300°F (this is important—don't wait until you're half done with the recipe).
3. Place pecans in zipper baggie and let children beat them with the wooden spoon to break into small pieces. Explain that after Jesus was arrested He was beaten by the Roman soldiers. Read John 19:1-3.
4. Let each child smell the vinegar. Put 1 tsp. vinegar into mixing bowl. Explain that when Jesus was thirsty on the cross He was given vinegar to drink. Read John 19:28-30.
5. Add egg whites to vinegar. Eggs represent life. Explain that Jesus gave His life to give us life. Read John 10:10, 11.
6. Sprinkle a little salt onto each child's hand. Let them taste it and brush the rest into the bowl. Explain that this represents

---

EASTER STORY COOKIE RECIPE (CONT.)

the salty tears shed by Jesus' followers and the bitterness of our own sin. Read Luke 23:27.

7. So far the ingredients are not very appetizing. Add 1 cup sugar. The sweet part of the story is that Jesus rose again. He died for our sins, and God raised Him from the dead. All those who believe on the Lord Jesus Christ shall be saved. Read Romans 4:22-25; Luke 24:6; Psalm 34:8; John 3:16.

8. Beat with a mixer on high speed for 12-15 minutes until stiff peaks form. Explain that the color of our sins is like scarlet, but when they are cleansed by Jesus they will be white like snow. The white color of the egg whites represents the cleansing of our sins. Read Isaiah 1:18 and John 3:1-3.

9. Fold in broken nuts. Drop by teaspoons onto a cookie sheet covered with wax paper. Explain that each mound represents the rocky tomb where Jesus' body was laid. Read Matthew 27:57-60.

10. Put the cookie sheet in the oven; close the door and turn the oven OFF. Do not bake the cookies!

11. Give each child a piece of tape and seal the oven door. Explain that Jesus' tomb was sealed. Read Matthew 27:65, 66.

12. GO TO BED! Explain that they may feel sad to leave the cookies in the oven overnight. Jesus' followers were in despair when the tomb was sealed. Read John 16:20, 22.

13. On Easter morning, open the oven and give everyone a cookie. Notice the cracked surface and take a bite. The cookies are hollow! On the first Easter Jesus' followers were amazed to find the tomb open and empty. Read Matthew 28:1-9.

Another Easter tradition the Hendricksons have is family home Communion on the Sabbath evening before Easter. I love this idea. In our travels between two churches we often miss out on Communion. Lora shared with me her recipe for Family Communion Bread. "Each ingredient in Communion (wine, whole-wheat flour, oil, salt, water, no leavening, bread) has biblical/spiritual significance," Lora told me. Having Communion at home with your children gives you ample time to answer all their questions and make the connections between the Communion items and their biblical or spiritual meaning.

My children have a favorite Easter tradition that I began when Josh was about three years old. It is called the Resurrection Eggs. I

LORA HENDRICKSON'S RECIPE FOR FAMILY COMMUNION BREAD

2 cups whole-wheat flour
½ cup oil
½ teaspoon salt
½ cup water

Mix together and roll thin on cookie sheet. Score into crackers with a knife. Bake at 350° F for about 15 minutes.

"To go along with our Communion (after foot washing), we talk about all seven elements of the bread and wine, looking up verses and thinking up all references we can think of to that particular element in the Bible: bread, leavening (or lack thereof), 'whole'-wheat flour (Mark 5, KJV), oil, salt, water, wine. Then we read the story of the Last Supper and have our bread and grape juice."
—*Lora Hendrickson*

recycled an egg carton to hold twelve plastic eggs, the kind you get at the drugstore and fill with Easter treats. So far, because my children are little and don't remember from year to year what is inside, the contents of my eggs have not changed since I originally filled them. Each one holds some small symbol of Easter: a length of purple thread (the royalty of Jesus), nails, a bit of wool, dried rose petals (Jesus is the Rose of Sharon), a piece of bread (Jesus is the Bread of Life), a tiny cross made from twigs and string. The last egg is always empty to signify the empty tomb.

Joshua and Rachel have to take turns picking up an egg, shaking it and trying to guess what's inside. Joshua remembers some of them now so next year I will change a few to keep him guessing. They enjoy this tradition so much that if I forget to mention it they bring it up themselves.

No one talked about the tradition of dying Easter eggs. I can't be the only one who does it. Though I have discovered through my friends that I perhaps practice the dying art of blowing the eggs rather than using hard-boiled ones. There really isn't much of a trick to this. Using a pin with a plastic head (because you have to push hard and a metal head will hurt your fingers more) you carefully pierce each end. I start with the end that will NOT be blown from because when you flip the egg over to do the other side it will begin to drip and I'm not crazy about anyone putting their mouth near raw egg considering the many dangers associated with it. I make a larger hole on the fatter side of the egg and a smaller hole on the narrow side. Then, blowing from the narrow end you force the contents of the eggs out into a bowl (or, if you are enterprising, you let your children do it because they love to and don't mind getting tingly cheeks from all that huffing and puffing).

There are many egg-dying kits on the market and you'll have no trouble finding one to suit your tastes, or you can experiment every year. I just recently learned that in France they don't bother with dyes. The children paint the eggs with watercolor. One year, when my birthday fell on Easter, some of my aunts painted a special egg for me using acrylic paints. I kept it for many years until it crumbled. You can spray the eggs with shellac to give them a little extra protection and gloss. My mother still has a basket of eggs made by my youngest sister before she left home. She uses them each year, storing them carefully, so she doesn't have to make more.

Which brings up the question of recycling. There's something about the fleeting nature of the celebration that lends itself to waste. Every year stores carry bags of plastic "grass" and piles of flimsy Easter baskets. I shudder to think of all that lot headed for the dump the Monday after Easter morning. It's easy to store Easter baskets (filled with their "grass") for use year after year. And if you do that you can justify spending a tiny bit more to get a decent basket. Part of the fun comes from decorating the baskets each year. You can use fabric and ribbons to give each basket a slightly different look. These materials can further be recycled for use in decorating gifts.

This year we displayed the eggs in a basket, but that was unsatisfactory since the children couldn't see **all** their creations at once. Next year I intend to harvest a sapling in the woods sometime in February and immerse it in water so it will sprout (and depending on the variety maybe even bloom) about Easter time. If we "plant" this in a bucket of sand it will make a great place to hang the eggs. A simple way to hang the blown eggs is to thread a ribbon through the holes. A knot or bead tied onto the bottom will keep the ribbon secure.

"At Easter time all the kids and grandkids get together for an Easter egg hunt which is very much enjoyed."
EVERETT ROBINSON

Other than a special breakfast I don't do much baking at Easter. I have memories of my mother making Hot Cross Buns to deliver to the neighbors. And there was usually a Lamb Cake (a cake in the shape of a lamb). Jeannie Fehl of Spartanburgh, S.C. shared an interesting culinary tradition. "I make Pitta Chiusa at Easter, which is an old Italian tradition in my family. It is a thin dough with a mixture of raisins and walnuts, red pepper, and oregano all rolled up like a snail and baked in the oven. Sounds unusual, but is really very good."

The most elaborate Easter tradition I received came from the Collier family. I'm anxious to try this program myself. "Easter is our biggest holiday," Vanessa wrote. "We begin at sunset on Good Friday. We invite friends and family. We serve dinner. Each thing that is served is related to the celebration: bread, grape juice, fruit, nuts, green vegetables, olives, roast lamb, broiled fish, eggs, bitter herbs, sweet sauce. The table is decorated with lilies, small stuffed sparrows (from local craft store) and candles.

"You are not allowed to serve yourself the meal, but someone else at the table must fill your plate. All conversation is about the emblems on the table and why we are remembering tonight in a special way and with these things: Jesus is the Bread of life; He is the Vine we are the branches; Creator of good things to eat (fruits, veggies, nuts); behold the lilies; not one sparrow falls; the Passover Lamb; the breakfast of fish, etc. This is creative and fun. Everyone participates. You can get very creative with the decorations. For example, little pieces of hay (born in a stable), red ribbons (by His stripes we are healed). As the meal progresses each person picks one object and explains something about Jesus' life. (The easy ones should be left for the small people at the table.)

"Sabbath, after church, we do our normal stuff—take a walk, spend time with friends, etc. When we return home we prepare eggs for the morning. We boil about two dozen. After they cool, the five of us sit at the table and think of all the blessings that God has given us. We write a blessing on each egg with wax crayons. Then my three children color the eggs and make a horrible mess (but they have a ball!). At sundown, worship is focused on how we don't often see God's blessings, like the disciples didn't see what was happening when Jesus died.

"The next morning Hubby and I hide 'God's blessings' in various spots. Then we wake the kids. They run around looking for eggs and scream 'I found God's Love,' 'I found God's Peace,' 'I found God's ...our dog Daisy,' etc. We just laugh and laugh!"

I knew you would all be interested in this special tradition so I asked Vanessa if I could share her entire Easter program and she graciously agreed. Here it is in full:

THE COLLIER'S EASTER PROGRAM

"This is the program we use after supper on Friday evening," says Vanessa. "Host 1 is my husband. I am Host 2. Guest readers can either read the passage or 'tell' the passage. 'Telling' the passage works much better when children are present. They can 'tell' the story without having to struggle with reading the words. Some passages should be left for adults to read, such as the Greatest Sacrifice section.

"Before each section begins the host/hostess should explain the symbols. For example in section one, The Creation, the green candle represents Creation. The green veggie dipped in saltwater signifies the Creator of all things: green fields and sea.

"I make up the salt water. The veggie I use is broccoli. For the white sauce I use the bitterest horseradish sauce I can find to signify the bitterness of sin. The red sauce is made from applesauce dyed red with grape jelly. I put in a spoon of extra sugar so it's really sweet. And I use matzo crackers for bread.

"As we start we tell everyone to break their cracker into four pieces. They are also given a copy of the program to read along. They need to know what response to make. Anyone not reading a part (such as small children) should be told to listen for the words 'Blessed is the name of the Lord.' When they hear that they should shout, 'Amen!'

"The thing I love about this is that it involves all of our five senses: taste, touch, hearing, smell, and sight. This is so important for little ones. Imagine a five-year-old with a mouth full of *bitter* horseradish that represents sin. It's something he won't want to try again.

"You'll need to have some candles ready. I use small Passover candles. (Even the candle colors represent part of the celebration. Example: 1 Green (Creation), 2 Purple/Black (sin), 3 Pink (shadowing of the Cross), 4 White (life of Christ), 5 Red/Black (His death that takes away sin), 6 Orange/Pink (the dawn of His resurrection), 7 Yellow/Gold (going home!). The neat thing about this is that as the passages are being read the first candles are getting smaller and smaller, by the time you're finished candles 1 and 2 are out (the sin candle has gone out)."

1. **THE CREATION**
   Guest Reader: Genesis 1:1–2:1.
   Host 1: Shout joyfully to the Lord, all the earth. Serve the Lord with gladness; come before Him with joyful singing.
   All: Know that the Lord Himself is God; It is He who has made us, and not we ourselves; We are His people and the sheep of His pasture.
   Host 2: Enter His gates with thanksgiving, and His courts with praise. Give thanks to Him; bless His name.
   All: For the Lord is good; His loving kindness is everlasting. And His faithfulness to all generations.

(Based on Psalm 100.)
Eat green vegetable, dipped in salt water
Guest Reader lights the green candle
Host 1: Praise the Lord our God—Creator of all things.
All: Blessed is the name of the Lord.

2. **THE FALL**
   Guest Reader: Genesis 2:8—3:24.
   Host 1: Create in me a pure heart, O God, and renew a steadfast
      spirit within me. Do not cast me from your presence or take
      your Holy Spirit away from me. Restore to me the joy of your
      salvation and grant me a willing spirit to sustain me.
   **All: Then I will teach transgressors Your ways, and sinners will
      turn back to You. Save me from bloodguilt, O God, the God
      who saves me, and my tongue will sing of Your
      righteousness.**
   Host 2: O Lord, open my lips, and my mouth will declare Your
      praise. You do not delight in sacrifice, or I would bring it; You
      do not take pleasure in burnt offerings.
   **All: The sacrifices of God are a broken spirit; a broken and
      contrite heart O God, You will not despise.**
      (Based on Psalm 51, in part.)
   Eat bread with white sauce.
   Guest Reader lights the purple/black candle.
   Host 1: Praise the Lord our God—merciful to sinners.
   All: Blessed is the name of the Lord.

3. **THE PROMISE**
   Guest Reader: Isaiah 52:11-53:12.
   Host 1: I will exalt You, my God the King; I will praise Your
      name forever and ever. Every day I will praise You and extol

Your name forever and ever.

All: Great is the Lord and most worthy of praise; His greatness no one can fathom. One generation will commend Your works to another; they will tell of Your mighty acts.

Host 2: They will celebrate Your abundant goodness and joyfully sing of Your righteousness. The Lord is gracious and compassionate, slow to anger and rich in love.

All: The Lord is faithful to all His promises and loving toward all He has made. The Lord upholds all those who fall and lifts up all who are bowed down.

Host 1: The eyes of all look to You, and You give them their food at the proper time. You open Your hand to satisfy the desires of every living thing.

All: The Lord is righteous in all His ways and loving toward all He has made. The Lord is near to all who call on Him, to all who call on Him in truth.

Host 2: He fulfills the desires of those who fear Him; He hears their cry and saves them. The Lord watches over all who love Him, but all the wicked He will destroy.

All: My mouth will speak in praise of the Lord. Let every creature praise His holy name forever and ever.

Eat bread with white sauce, covered with red.

Guest Reader lights the pink candle.

Host 1: Praise the Lord our God for His plan of redemption.

All: Blessed is the name of the Lord.

4. THE MESSIAH

Guest Reader: Matthew 1:18-2:23.

All: Sharing of texts/passages on the ministry and mission of Christ. *

Host 1: In this the love of God was manifested toward us, that

God has sent His only begotten Son into the world, that we might live through Him.

All: "For God did not send His Son into the world to condemn the world, but that the world through Him might be saved."

Host 2: In this is love, not that we loved God, but that He loved us and sent His Son to be the propitiation for our sins.

All: God is love, and he who abides in love abides in God, and God in him.

(From 1 John 4 and John 3.)

Eat bread with red sauce.

Guest Reader lights white candle.

Host 1: Praise the Lord our God, who always keeps His promises.

All: Blessed is the name of the Lord.

5. **THE GREATEST SACRIFICE**

Guest Reader 1: John 13:1-11.

Guest Reader 2: Matthew 26:20-30.

Guest Reader 3: John 18:1-19:42.

Host 1 lights the red or black candle.

Prayer (Lead by hosts and followed by any who wish. Ended by hosts.)

Host 1: Praise the Lord our God—the suffering Lamb which takes away the sin of the world.

All: Blessed is the name of the Lord.

6. **RESURRECTION**

Guest Reader: John 20.

Host 1: After the Lord Jesus had spoken to them, He was taken up into heaven and He sat at the right hand of God.

Host 2: If Christ has not been raised, our preaching is useless and so is your faith...but, Christ has indeed been raised from the dead, the first fruits of those who have fallen asleep.

(From Mark 16 and 1 Corinthians 15.)

Host 1: Praise the Lord, O my soul; with my innermost being, praise His holy name. Praise the Lord, O my soul and forget not all His benefits.

All: He forgives all my sins and heals all my diseases; He redeems my life from the pit and crowns me with love and compassion. He satisfies my desires with good things, so that my youth is renewed like the eagle's.

Host 2: The Lord is compassionate and gracious, slow to anger, abounding in love…He does not treat us as our sins deserve or repay us according to our iniquities.

All: For as high as the heavens are above the earth, so great is His love for those who fear Him; as far as the east is from the west, so far has He removed our transgressions from us. Praise the Lord, O my soul!

(From Psalm 103.)

Eat bread, drink "wine."

Guest Reader lights orange/pink candle.

Host 1: Praise the Lord our God, intercessing High Priest in heaven's temple.

All: Blessed is the name of the Lord.

7. **THE RETURN**

Guest Reader: John 14:1-4.

Host 1: I looked and there before me was a great multitude that no one could count, from every nation, tribe, people, and language, standing before the throne and in front of the Lamb. They were wearing white robes and were holding palm branches in their hands.

All: And they cried out in a loud voice; "Salvation belongs to our God, who sits on the throne, and to the Lamb."

Host 2: All the angels were standing around the throne and around the elders and the four living creatures. They fell down on their faces before the throne and worshiped God saying:

All: "Amen! Praise and glory and wisdom and thanks and honor and power and strength be to our God forever and ever. Amen!"

Host 1: Then one of the elders asked me, "These in white robes—who are they, and where did they come from?" I answered, "Sir, you know." And he said, "These are they who have come out of the great Tribulation; they have washed their robes and made them white in the blood of the Lamb. Therefore,

All: "They are before the throne of God and serve Him day and night in His temple; and He who sits on the throne will spread His tent over them.

Host 2: "Never again will they hunger; never again will they thirst. The sun will not beat down upon them, nor any scorching heat.

All: "For the Lamb at the center of the throne will be their Shepherd; He will lead to springs of living water. And God will wipe away every tear from their eyes."

(From Revelation 7.)

Host 1: Praise the Lord our God, who is coming again soon.

All: Blessed is the name of the Lord.

* "Everyone shares texts that they have memorized and/or are personal texts/stories," explains Vanessa. "For example, I love the passage that talks about when Jesus heals the leper. The leper comes to Jesus and says, 'If You want to You can make me clean,' and Jesus says, 'I want to; be clean.' I think about that passage a lot, because I

want Jesus to make me clean too. Or someone might paraphrase a text. 'In My Father's house are many mansions, and I go to prepare a place for you.' This gives me hope in Jesus' soon return. The object is to share a passage that makes the gospel real to you."

(The responsive readings are adapted or taken from the readings in *The SDA Hymnal.*)

No matter how you celebrate Easter its message is one of the most important we can hear all year. "Arise, shine; for your light has come! And the glory of the Lord is risen upon you. For behold, the darkness shall cover the earth, and deep darkness the people; but the Lord will arise over you, and His glory will be seen upon you. The Gentiles shall come to your light, and kings to the brightness of your rising" (Isaiah 60:1-3, NKJV).

CHAPTER FOUR

May Day

I confess I don't know much about May Day. In fact, I wasn't even sure it was celebrated on May 1ˢᵗ until I looked it up. I had a vague impression of May poles and flowers, but had no idea that May 1 in some countries is an international holiday to celebrate labor organizations. Overlooking its labor union associations and its possible pagan origins, May Day is first and foremost a time to celebrate renewal of life. Following Easter as closely as it does, it seems a perfect time to do this.

Diane Pearson, Dean of Women at Walla Walla College, has a unique way of celebrating this day, "After World War II our family lived in a housing project, row upon row of houses, similar to townhouses of today. Before May Day my mother would help us children make cone-shaped colored paper May baskets with paper handles. The handles were looped enough to fit over a doorknob. On May Day morning we would fill them with flowers, go door to door in the housing project, hang a basket on a doorknob, knock on the door, and run to the next house. It was gratifying to do something for others without thought of reward. The warm feeling bubbled inside each of us!"

Though I've never delivered flowers surreptitiously on May Day, I have done so at other times during the year. I like Martha Stewart's idea of making a little basket from an old tin can. After washing, remove the label. Pound a nail near the top lip on opposite sides of the can. Using wire, string a handle. If you want, you can paint these a Shabby Chic look, but they're interesting plain. Put a little water in the bottom and fill with wildflowers if they are available or the store bought variety if nothing is in bloom on May 1.

These little bouquets are generally known as tussie mussies. Victorian ladies used to fill small cone vases with bouquets of flowers. The vases became known as *Tussie-Mussie* holders: *tussie* meaning a knot of flowers and *mussie* for the moist moss that kept the flowers fresh. Tussie mussie holders can be made with many materials. I've heard of spray painting ice-cream cones copper or gold and filling them with silk flowers. With a ribbon glued on they can be hung from a window or doorknob. (These even make a nice Christmas tree decoration.) Or you can make a paper cone to carry your blooms in.

I like the idea that May Day, whatever its origins or associations, can be used to brighten the lives of people we care about and those who may be lonely. "We celebrate May Day," Donita Culbertson told me. "My hubby's grandpa gave flowers to his grandma every year for over sixty years! My husband and/or kids have gone to great lengths to deliver flowers. They have hidden on the porch roof and beside our cars. Once Hubby even shinnied (he's 6'5") out a basement window, crawled past the kitchen window where I was making a meal and to the front door bell to deliver! Our youngest son and I have taken pansies or petunias to family/friends of his choice for six May days. I collect 6-10 little baskets at the Salvation Army and we purchase plants and load up the van. A couple times his friends have gone with us too."

I hope that like me you have glimpsed the possibilities of May Day. The next time it rolls around I know I'll be thinking of Diane and the Culbertsons and using their ideas to brighten the days of people I know. Don't be too surprised if you, too, hear a knock on the door and find when you answer an empty doorstep, but lovely blooms swaying slightly from the doorknob. You never know which one of your acquaintances might be taken with the idea of drive-by flowering. Who knows, the idea could catch on. Think of how many lives would be brightened then; even more so, with a Scripture note attached to the handle of the basket. Here's one for you to try out:

" ' " 'The Lord bless you and keep you; the Lord make His face shine upon you, and be gracious to you; the Lord lift up His countenance upon you, and give you peace' " ' " (Numbers 6:24-26, NKJV).

CHAPTER FIVE

Halloween

I call Halloween the un-holiday. I received more traditions for **not** celebrating Halloween than for celebrating it. And I can't say that it either surprised me or disappointed me. I had problems with Halloween early on, though, like most holidays I didn't really have to act on them until I had children. We live far enough off the road that we've never had a single trick-or-treater to worry about. I have never "decorated" for Halloween and really didn't give it much thought until the children got old enough to realize something was going on that night and they weren't a part of it.

I loved your suggestions for alternative activities because I think that no matter how hard we try to convince our kids otherwise they know they're missing out on something. I don't have great associations with trick-or-treating myself. Sure, I loved getting to dress up and I loved getting candy, but being a shy child it was torture to go around, knock on doors and say, "Trick or treat."

And it wasn't because they were the doors of strangers. These were all people I knew. We only went around to the houses on our dead-end road. The one house I remember being interested in going to was the one where a Chinese family lived. They had the most interesting decorations, like nothing I'd ever seen before, and they always led us on a tour through the house.

When it came time I knew I didn't want my kids trick-or-treating. Besides the issues about what Halloween is all about, there were health considerations. It's not exactly a safe thing to do any more. But, the crux of the matter is, What are we celebrating here? I haven't been able to find one good thing about Halloween.

So, instead we celebrate Harvest, which, coincidentally takes place about the same time of year and is an actual, legitimate festivity. Usually one of the homeschool families hosts a Harvest Party and the kids can dress up in costumes. It's understood that they shouldn't be costumes of witches, devils, or other objectionable characters. The kids get enough candy to keep them satisfied, but not too much.

---

*"Halloween we try to ignore as much as possible.
If we get ghosts or goblins at our door we give them
a healthy treat wrapped up with a little booklet
about the love of God."*
THE JAY THOMAS FAMILY

In the past we've hung donuts from the ceiling and had the kids try to eat them without touching them. We've bobbed for apples and had other fun little activities for them to do. Susan Maxted of College Place, Washington has a great family tradition to take the place of Halloween. "On Halloween all the family that is in town gathers at Grandma and Grandpa's house for a donut party. The grandchildren look forward to helping make donuts. Several different glazes are made and they decorate some. After the donuts are done they sit back and watch the same video every year and eat donuts. They now bring friends over to help."

Some families like to get out of their house on Halloween night to avoid the hordes of trick-or-treaters that come knocking at the door. Julie Kaas's family found a great place to escape to. "Not wanting to participate in any way with Halloween, we decided to go spend the night at a local hotel that has an indoor swimming pool. In the morning we go out to breakfast. It is a little expensive but well worth it!"

Tammy Cantrell's family found a similar solution. "We do not celebrate Halloween in our home for several reasons one of which was that we didn't want the kids to feel like they were only being deprived of 'candy stashes' for the next three months. So, every year on Halloween for the last ten years we have gone to a store and let them pick out a big bag of candy. They choose where we eat supper and then we go to a movie (that way we don't have to answer the door either and have them be reminded of what they're missing!). In the end, the only thing they really want is the candy!"

Charles Reel found a delicious excuse to be away from home on Halloween evening. "Our children are twenty-two months old and four years old," Charles says. "Neither my wife nor I are big supporters of Halloween. In fact we don't like all the ghost, monsters, and satanic overtones it has. We also don't care for the kids dressing up as these characters and then getting candy from everyone. We live in a subdivision and last year we did something that we are planning to continue as a tradition. We have some friends from church who live out away from the city. Last year we got together with them and had a homemade ice-cream party.

"This year we did it again with a few more people. It is great because this couple has grown children and they make great local 'grandparents' to our kids. Since we have no family in the area it is just fun to have a place to get away from all the Halloween hype. This couple also has an old player piano that is fun to play. This is something we felt was a good alternative for our kids to do and still have fun without all the Halloween hype."

While it's fun to host a party yourself, if that sounds like too much work it's possible you may already have a ready-made alternative close to home. "This year another Protestant church had a wonderful Harvest Party," Ardie Earhart told me. "They got support from many local businesses and set up all kinds of things at our county fairgrounds. There were games, Bible stories, animals, a petting zoo, pony rides, eats, and even a climbing wall. All the people in charge were dressed in biblical costumes. It was a great success!"

Some families use Halloween as an outreach program. My first inclination is to hide from what's going on around me or do something, anything, else, but Laura Ames meets Halloween head on, bringing happiness to those who are less fortunate.

"During the month of October we baked cookies," she told me. "A favorite one we've discovered is apple, raisin, and nut spice. We put them in sandwich bags and tied them with fall-colored ribbons (the curly kind). Then we put them in the freezer in a container. For Halloween our daughter would dress up in a 'could-be-true' outfit, like a nurse, an angel, pumpkin—nothing wild. We would invite a friend to go with us to an elderly-people's residential apartment building. The girls would knock on doors and say 'Trick or Treat. Here's your treat' and then hand them a package of cookies. Then they would sing a 'Jesus song' for them.

"The old people loved it! After we did it a couple of years they got so they waited for the girls to come. It was a blessing for the girls also. They had fun making others happy and we were not honoring Satan on Halloween. It also helped to avoid the 'I wish I could go out like the other kids.' "

I like the idea of taking a proactive stand against Halloween without being offensive about it. I'll admit I *feel* offensive when I think about Halloween, which could be the biggest reason I have trouble thinking up positive solutions to the dilemma of what to do *instead*. While I don't have to deal with children showing up on my doorstep on Halloween some of you must. I received some excellent suggestions about how to minister to these little folk.

"Some years back I folded up the stack of extra *Our Little Friend*s and *Primary Treasure*s left over each week at my church," Faith Laughlin wrote. "I folded them in the classic tri-fold popular with many SDA Sabbath School departments and then I filled the 'pocket' with candies, etc. I dressed up my eldest, about fifteen months old, in a costume and gleefully passed them out to the neighborhood children. If any parents from the shadows behind the kids asked about the papers I just smiled and explained that as a teacher I had to give some good stories to read as brain food."

I don't know about you, but I think use by one single family seems like a tragic waste of potential for our magazines. Recycling them as treats at Halloween is an excellent use of our resources and a tremendous blessing to the kids who receive them. "One year when the children were small," Sandra Cruz told me, "we wrapped up the Halloween issue of *Our Little Friend* in orange and black tissue paper, and gave those out to children. Some said it was better than candy because they got candy at all the other houses. One boy said it was the only thing he owned to read that was his."

Another terrific magazine to deliver as treats during Halloween is *Winner,* our drug and alcohol prevention magazine for younger readers. If you order back issues it's really cost effective and so much better for kids than candy. To inquire about rates and available issues call Ron Clark, Director for Listen-Winner Sales at 1-800-548-8700, ext.3177.

---

*"We have always gone to a special place for dinner
or some fun out of the house activity."*
JEANNIE FEHL, SPARTANBURGH, S.C.

It doesn't matter where you live, down the block or down under. If you are in a populated area chances are you'll have to figure out what to do about the trick-or-treaters, even if it's simply turning off all the lights and lying low for the night. "Halloween is one of those holidays you wish didn't exist, but can't avoid," Judi Larsen wrote to me from New Zealand. "The junk mail and TV is full of it. I've explained to my kids that it's not something we want anything to do with, but then you get kids knocking on your door all evening. That's not something you can avoid, and I always give them something, because they are usually neighborhood kids and not usually as awful as they look in their witch's costumes!"

Let's face it, the two big draws at Halloween are the costumes and the candy. There's a lot you can do with those two items that have nothing to do with Halloween. My friend Deb Foote sent me an idea for a costume party that her husband cooked up. "Dave did a neat thing for Halloween about fifteen years ago in Pathfinders. We wanted to have a party where they could kind of dress up, but not ghoulish. So he had a hat costume party. It was really interesting. I still have the picture of Jamie, at age nine years old with his decorated flower pot on his head."

Sometimes the way you celebrate (or don't celebrate) something evolves over time. Lora Hendrickson of Pendleton, Oregon described to me how her tradition changed as her convictions about the holiday changed. "We used to have a party with my sister and family, but now since neither of us live in a normal neighborhood (no trick-or-treaters), we can ignore it. However, this year we had special friends for dinner that evening, and at other times we may have a special activity as a family. The kids know about Halloween, we do talk about it, but we do not celebrate it. And our extended family members have grown to understand.

"When we lived in town, though, and thought compromise was OK, I allowed our kids to dress in Bible or animal costumes, and gave away *Our Little Friend* Sabbath School papers with candy. We visited some old friends who didn't ignore Halloween and took them a surprise. Of course that meant our kids got candy.

"For the most part we ignore Halloween. People ask the children, 'Are you going trick-or-treating? What are you going to dress up like? Did you know they have a huge free party for kids at the Convention Center?' A new tradition for us is to ask our children after such question-asking sessions, 'How does it make you feel when people talk about Halloween?' We find out they do not feel they are missing out on anything.

"We talk a lot about why the parents in this family take a stand on certain issues, and try to answer questions if the children don't understand. This year our eight-year-old asked his eleven-year-old brother, 'What does Halloween celebrate?' The answer he got ('Satan') settled his mind on why we do not celebrate the day. We celebrate what is worthy of celebrating."

I won't deny that how you celebrate or don't celebrate Halloween is a controversial subject. We have many ways to meet this dilemma and I'm thankful to see that people more creative than myself have discovered ways to not only deal with it, but to use it to spread the joy of Jesus to others. No matter what holiday we're celebrating, that should be our ultimate aim anyway.

CHAPTER SIX

Thanksgiving

Thanksgiving. Just that one word conjures up so many memories, all of them revolving around the delicious smells coming from Grandma Perrino's kitchen. We'd congregate in the living room, reading the funnies or watching an old movie on television. The grown-ups would talk current events while stomachs began to rumble. But, my grandmother had a talent for entertaining. Everything was timed perfectly. We never waited long before she called us to the table. The food was served so quickly it was like slight of hand. You almost expected to see waiters materialize at your elbow, but they never did.

The menu was as much a tradition as forgetting the coleslaw out in the breezeway where it was being kept cool. We had the standard Thanksgiving fare, my favorite being the candied sweet potatoes. I don't know how long she baked beforehand, but there was always an abundance of desserts crowding the shelf in addition to the meal.

GRANDMA PERRINO'S CANDIED SWEET POTATOES

6 sweet potatoes
¼ cup butter
½ tsp. salt
½ cup brown sugar, packed
¼ cup chopped pecans

Wash potatoes. Cover with water and boil until tender. Drain.
Cool. In skillet, combine remaining ingredients. Stir over low
heat until butter melts and sugar is dissolved. Boil 3 minutes.
Reduce heat and add potatoes. Baste while simmering. Serve hot.

SWEET POTATO AND APPLE SCALLOP

If you'd like to try an alternative version of sweet potatoes,
I offer my sister Faith's recipe, which is also wonderful.

2 cups thinly sliced, boiled sweet potatoes
2 cups peeled, thinly sliced, tart apples
½ cup brown sugar
4 Tbs. butter
Salt

Grease casserole dish. Begin layering in this order: half of the
potatoes, half the apples, half the brown sugar, half the butter and
half the salt. Repeat. Bake covered at 350° F for 30 minutes.
Uncover and continue to bake another 30 minutes or until apples
are soft.

Though my memories center around my grandmother's table, my children's memories center around my mother's. The food is the same, but with the shift in location I found I had some unexpected adjusting to do. One of the drawbacks of having traditions is that it can be hard to accept a change. Eventually change comes to us all. But, having traditions in place does make the transition easier.

Seventeen-year-old Jessica Dorval wrote to tell me how her family coped with difficult times over the holidays. "Many times Thanksgiving is a holiday that gets overlooked because of the anticipation for Christmas. But for my family, one our most memorable traditions is centered around this holiday. About five years ago my family was going through some very stressful times. Not just in my immediate family, but the whole lot of us. I was only twelve at the time, but I could feel the stress mounting as the leaves turned colors, and a chill went through the Nebraska air.

"Thanksgiving was approaching, and we didn't feel very thankful at all. My Dad with wisdom beyond his years, came up with a simple suggestion to put us in the right mood, and thus started a much needed family tradition. When the day came and everyone was seated around the table in my grandparent's dining room with the lights dimmed, my father produced twenty-four white taper candles. He divided the candles and passed them to the left and to the right. He then struck a match and lit his candle. He explained to us that Thanksgiving was a time to be thankful, to cherish those around you, and to remember how God has provided for you throughout the year—despite the stressful days, or weeks, or months. He then told what he was thankful for, and turned to the left and lit my mother's candle. She, wiping her eyes, told what she was thankful for, and soon, the whole room was illuminated with the light from our candles.

"Our whole family was truly blessed that day. And ever since, it has been the most memorable family tradition. It has helped us to reflect on how much God has blessed us, and how we can help others who are less fortunate than us. I look forward to this every year, and it makes me feel special because it's a time to tell my family how much I love them. I'm very thankful to God that I have them as my family."

As you would expect, the main components of a Thanksgiving celebration are giving thanks, food, family, and friends. This section includes some terrific recipes that I hope you'll try. Maybe you'll find one that will become a part of your annual Thanksgiving table. Take Cris Cannuli Dorval's cranberry relish recipe for example.

"Our family has exponentially grown over the years," Cris says, "but we continue to try to get together for Thanksgiving and Christmas, regardless of the size. This Thanksgiving (just a few days ago) we packed twenty-seven at my sister's dining-room table. One simple recipe that has not been forgotten in all of my thirty-four years of Thanksgivings is Cranberry Relish. It is a very easy recipe to make, and is special to us."

There are some recipes that simply **must** be on the Thanksgiving table or the meal would not be complete. Julie Voth's family came up with a creative way to help everyone feel included in the Thanksgiving meal. "When our original family started adding spouses we made Thanksgiving a 'potluck' with each spouse contributing their 'It's-not-Thanksgiving-without-_____' dish. We didn't know how meaningful this would become. Not only does it provide various comfort foods for those not with their family of origin but looking at the table gives proof of our blended families and the new family we've become. Many of the spouses' contributions have become firm and fast parts of our own meal, even when they're not there!"

I've yet to be called upon to make an entire Thanksgiving meal, though I have cooked contributions for the city mission which presents a Thanksgiving dinner to the less fortunate in our area. I

CRIS CANNULI DORVAL'S CRANBERRY RELISH

1 bag cranberries
¾–1 cup sugar (to taste, and natural sugar works great)
3–4 large Cortland apples (or you can use any sweet apple)
2 10.5-oz cans mandarin oranges, drained
1 cup walnuts

Sort and rinse cranberries. Shred them in a food processor, being careful not to mince them too small. Put in medium to large bowl. Peel and shred apples. Add to the cranberries. Stir in 1/2 cup of sugar, check to see if sweet enough, and continue adding until desired sweetness. (The size and sweetness of the apples makes it different every time.) Finally, add the drained mandarin oranges and walnuts, and gently toss together. The flavors meld together the longer it sits, so it's nice to have it made about a day in advance to serving. Enjoy!

have a vague idea that someone preparing the entire meal probably starts at least a week in advance. Someday I'll probably find out the hard way. In the meantime, I'm content to contribute a dish when I get the chance. Next year I might try Stephanie's Great-Grammie's Dinner Rolls. They sound wonderful.

"My seventeen-year-old daughter, Stephanie, has the touch, as far as baking goes," her mother Christine Greene told me. "She started baking her great-grammie's dinner rolls for special occasions. She has made them a few times, and did them for the Thanksgiving Dinner here at our office (Columbia Union) where they were a big hit. She also makes and sells them to the neighbors. We enjoy them as well, and look forward to the tradition of Great-Grammie's Dinner Rolls,

GREAT-GRAMMIE'S DINNER ROLLS

1 cup water (warm) or milk, scalded
¼ cup oil or shortening
¼ cup honey or sugar
1 egg, slightly beaten
1 Tbs. yeast, dissolved in ¼ cup warm water (adding honey
    makes it rise faster)
3 ½ cups sifted all-purpose flour
Pinch of salt

In a large bowl combine flour, sugar, shortening, salt. Add dissolved yeast, egg, and 2 cups of the flour. Add water. Gradually add remaining flour. Stir together into soft dough. Cover. Let rise for 1 ½ hours. Punch down (great stress reducer)! Turn out on board, knead a little, add a little bit of flour, knead some more. Shape as desired (little balls for dinner rolls). Let rise in pans (cover lightly with dishtowel while they rise). Bake at 400°F for 15 minutes.

even though Great-Grammie passed away a few years ago. We still enjoy the wonderful flavor for special occasions and remember past times with all the family, excellent dinner rolls, butter and jam!"

Having to travel two hours to be with family on Thanksgiving, I sympathize with others who are torn between travel and starting their own traditions at home. Traveling a great deal around the holidays is stressful and too much of it can ruin the holiday spirit we're trying to cultivate. But, it's a difficult decision to make. Ties to family are strong, particularly this time of year. Usually a compromise can be reached, maybe with holidays being traded off or celebrated at a less hectic time. Kimberly Harris shared her struggle with me.

"This is a Thanksgiving family tradition that we are beginning this year. Because Thanksgiving and Christmas are so close, we have found that all of the rushing from here to there to visit his parents and my parents, and whatever other family reunions and parties arise at that time of year, leaves us worn out and rushed. Rather than enjoying the holidays, we dread the chaos. So we've elected to spend Thanksgiving every year at home, or at least near home, and not with our parents. This year, we are having dinner with a cousin, but in future years we intend to invite old friends, new friends, no friends, or whatever suits us. We seek to minister on that day to our friends, or to our immediate family, letting them know how thankful we are that they are part of our lives."

Holidays can become a battleground if we're not careful. Many a hapless couple spends them in agony trying to fulfill unrealistic family expectations. It makes sense early on to decide how best to incorporate both sides of the extended family. If they are located close together it may be possible to have a holiday breakfast with one and supper with the other. Or maybe like Kimberly you would rather spend one holiday alone and share another.

Whatever you do, however you work it out, it's important that one family doesn't feel slighted at the expense of the other. I've seen the results of this first hand and it creates resentments and frustration that run very deep indeed.

If your family is very large you might want to consider renting a place like Everett Robinson's family does. "I married a girl from a very large family known as the Byrds of Hagerstown, MD," Everett told me. "Her name is Annadell (Byrd) Robinson and she is the 5th child of 6 (3 girls and 3 boys). Well, one of our 'Family Traditions' is that every Thanksgiving Day all the brothers and sisters and their family along with the grandkids rent the Mt. Aetna Elementary school gym in Hagerstown, MD, and we have our annual Thanksgiving Day dinner together. Everyone brings a selected 'dish' and we go 'potluck.' After that we play basketball and volleyball and have a great time together. This we have done for many, many years now. We number about 50+ at present."

ANITA'S CRANBERRY SALAD
"This is a favorite recipe that our family looks forward to each Thanksgiving."—Anita Jacobs.

1 12-oz. package raw cranberries
1 ¾ cup white sugar
1 cup chopped pecans
1 cup red seedless grapes, cut in quarters
½ pint whipping cream

Grind cranberries, add sugar. When sugar has dissolved, add pecans and grapes. Mix together with cranberry/sugar mixture. Whip cream until soft peaks; fold into cranberry mixture. Place in a pretty clear glass bowl. Enjoy!

When I became involved in historical re-enacting of the eighteenth century I learned a lot about the early settlers and found out that some of what we think of as "history" connected with our traditions isn't historically accurate. It can be fun to gain a deeper understanding of our traditions, especially for children. A good place to start is on the Internet at the site of the Plimoth Plantation, which can be found at **www.plimoth.org**. They have a lot of information about the many complex issues involved as well as foods similar to ones that might have been served at the first Thanksgiving.

"Memories are the bread of life."
CHRISTINE GREENE

Tony Zbaraschuk sent me an interesting tradition. "At Thanksgiving, my father would read from William Bradford's account of the establishment of Plymouth and the first Thanksgiving service. Quite moving. Not sure where he found it—he's been doing it ever since I can recall. The text gets printed every year in the Wall Street Journal around Thanksgiving time, I believe, but the account could have been from almost anywhere; it's one of the classic accounts of the pilgrim's settlement in New England. Still ongoing, still deeply moving."

Though I can't be sure, I think the account Tony's father read came from William Bradford's book titled, *Of Plymouth Plantation,* an important historical text which is required reading in many high school and college American Literature courses.

"We have collected various Thanksgiving books which we've read every year," Lora Hendrickson told me, "including activity books and projects. You have to really look, but they are out there. We found a pilgrim and Indian figure set and put it out much like we do the Nativity scene later.

"This year for Thanksgiving we read our usual round of books out loud together throughout the month of November. This year our quest was to figure out what parts of these books are accurate or not. There are a lot of made-up stories and parts of stories; many conflict with one another. We did an Internet search and learned a lot about what really did happen, got a copy of the Mayflower Compact, learned exactly who were those pilgrims on the Mayflower and as much as we could about them. It is a good way to learn the difference between historical fiction, accurate historical accounts, and fanciful writing.

"Another tradition we have is that before we eat our meal, we each have three kernels of corn to remember what we are thankful for. Each kernel represents one thing. We pick up a kernel and share with the rest of the family what we are thankful for, place it back on the plate in a new place, and take up the second kernel, etc. It is a good time for us to really be thankful (and not just gluttonous). We are able to appreciate each other and God out loud that way too."

Many people shared with me various creative ways to express our thanks during this thank-filled holiday. My family does not yet have a tradition like this and I'd like to incorporate one. Ernie Medina, Jr. told me about a clever way his family has created to remember their blessings.

"One of our more unique Thanksgiving traditions is that we have a Thank You Jar that we keep in the kitchen. Every time something that we're thankful for happens, we write it on a piece of colored paper, fold it up, and put it in the jar. Then on Thanksgiving Day, we go through the jar and remember all the times that we have to be thankful for. It's a yearlong activity, so it's neat to sit down once a year and go through all of our thankful events, many of which we have forgotten. This coming Thanksgiving will be our second year doing this. We started this last year when our daughter had just turned two and we wanted to start a unique family tradition that was new to both of us."

Rhonda Martin records blessings in a journal. "Throughout the year we write blessings, answered prayers and miracle stories that we experience in a special burgundy velvet covered journal. At the Thanksgiving table each year we read the stories from the current year, and years past, to remember all the things for which we are thankful. This tradition began one year as we found ourselves feeling quite grateful for many things, but at a real loss for words. Our journal of blessings enables us to relive the presence of God in our lives throughout the year with great passion, emotion and detail. This tradition enriches our Thanksgiving and creates a written legacy of God's divine hand in our day-to-day lives. It is becoming a precious heirloom."

Most of us have countless blessings, but when we try to remember exactly what they are, the passage of time has blurred them. That's why recording them this way is so helpful. Not only does writing our blessings down give us a record so we don't forget, it also shows us, concretely, how God is working in our lives.

"One Thanksgiving, before dinner, we were going around the room trying to remember things that had occurred that year that we were thankful for," Jeannie Fehl told me. "We surely couldn't remember them all for the whole year. So, now, every Saturday we write in a little book about the things we are thankful for, for that week. On Thanksgiving Day we open the book and reflect on the year's happenings."

Kathy Phillips's family celebrates their Thanksgiving and Christmas in a creative way.

"Our favorite holiday (Christmas and Thanksgiving) activity was to make egg salad sandwiches and spend the day water skiing thus outsmarting the tropic heat. We could have the usual holiday menu of mock turkey roast, cranberries, pies, etc. for Sabbath lunch any time of the year."

When Nancy Johnson of Manton, Michigan wrote to tell me of her family's special Thanksgiving tradition I was immediately reminded of a cabin in Maine I used to love. It belonged to the people I stayed with while I was going to Pine Tree Academy. While I was there they made a couple trips to the cabin and I loved every minute of it. I can still smell the butternut squash, scooped out and filled with butter and cayenne pepper and baked. And I can still hear the rain pattering on the roof. Cabins are special places.

JEAN BOONSTRA'S THANKSGIVING PIE

"I have my own traditional Thanksgiving/Christmas Pie recipe for a vegetarian main entrée. I have modified the original recipe each year for a few years, and now I think I've perfected it!"—Jean E. Boonstra.

6 cups whole-wheat bread, cubed
1 Tbs. canola oil
1 cup diced onion
Garlic clove, crushed
Rib of celery, finely diced
¾ cup finely diced fresh mushrooms
Carrot, shredded
1 cup peeled and shredded tart apple
1 tsp. dried thyme
1 tsp. dried parsley
1 tsp. poultry seasoning (contains no meat)
1½ cup G Washington's golden vegetable broth
1½ cup chicken style gravy (homemade or packaged)
Worthington frozen turkey slices (approx. 10)
Pie pastry (enough for a traditional double crust pie)

Preheat oven to 375°F.

Preparing dressing: The night before, dice bread and leave out on cookie sheets to dry.

Heat oil in a nonstick frying pan. Sauté onion, garlic, and celery lightly over medium heat. Once celery has softened slightly, add mushrooms and carrot. Continue to sauté until mushrooms are soft. Add thyme, parsley, and poultry seasoning. Stir apple into sautéed mixture, and leave on heat just long enough to heat apple through.

Transfer sautéed mixture to large mixing bowl. Add diced bread cubes and stir with wooden spoon to mix. Boil water and add broth package. I find it easiest to do this in a glass measuring cup so that adding the broth to the dry mixture is easier.

Add broth to the dry bread mixture about a ¼ cup at a time. Mix well with wooden spoon. Depending on how moist or dry you like your dressing, you may or may not use the whole 1½ cups of broth.

Assembling pie: Prepare your favorite pie pastry recipe. Divide pastry into 2 portions, one ¾ and the other ¼ of the dough. Roll out larger portion on a floured surface. Line a flatdish with the pastry.

Prepare gravy. With a brush, brush the bottom of the pie with part of the gravy.

1st layer: Half of the turkey slices, cut in half. Brush tops of slices with gravy.

2nd layer: Dressing mixture. Press down with the back of the wooden spoon.

3rd layer: The remainder of the turkey slices. Brush with gravy.

4th layer: Dressing mixture. Enough to come to the top of your dish. You will *not* use all of it.

Put the leftover dressing in a greased casserole dish and put in oven, once the heat has been reduced, to bake along with the pie. Roll out the remaining pastry. With a cookie cutter cut out festive shapes. For Thanksgiving leaves are nice. Arrange on the top of the pie.

Bake pie for 15 minutes at 375°F, then reduce temperature to 325°F and bake for 20-30 minutes more.

"I have been married for almost thirty-eight years," Nancy told me. "When I married my husband, he and all of his family, including his mother hunted deer during the last two weeks of November in Michigan. So Thanksgiving dinner was soup kept warm on the wood stove in the old hunting cabin. Very, very rustic, rough, old cabin! This cabin has been in the family for three generations and still has no electricity.

"I was surprised by this lack of desire to set down to the big festive dinner. So I would prepare dinner in my kitchen from the main course right down to the pumpkin pie, pack it all into the car along with the dishes to serve it on and head for the cabin. Mom, Dad, and Jack, my husband, would come in around two o'clock for dinner. Our daughters loved going to the cabin for dinner too. It became a family tradition that went astray for several years. Well, the old cabin now belongs to Jack and me and we are now taking dinner back to the cabin for all of the family on Thanksgiving. Dad has passed away but Mom ... she really enjoys the memories."

Because I've never been in charge of the Thanksgiving meal, I've never had the opportunity to invite the less fortunate to my table. I've brought food to them, as I said before, but that doesn't seem like the same thing. I greatly admire those who invite others to share Thanksgiving with their families. I am sure they receive a great blessing from it.

"I fondly remember Thanksgivings," Dixie Plata told me. "Weather permitting we kids spent the morning with Dad in the yard raking the last of the leaves, putting straw around plants and trees and getting ready for winter. Then we would come in the warm house and eat the good food Mother had prepared. The part that made it special is that we always had guests, usually a homeless person or hobo, who seemed to know that our home was a good stopping place. We met some very interesting people that way and learned how special it is to share what we have even though it was never fancy."

Alison B. Carleton, a doctor in Iowa, and her family share their Thanksgiving meal with friends who have become like the family they miss. "On Thanksgiving a couple from church whose kids are out of state come over. This couple has kids our age who live out of state; so do our folks. We enjoy each other a lot. And they like the chance to act as grandparents to our kids.

"We started getting together with them each year. I always make a stuffing FriChik® dressing, which is easy, and pumpkin pie. We're always trying to be healthy. This year I used the recipe I got from 3ABN and it was good."

DR. CARLETON'S EASY FRICHIK® DRESSING

Mix seasoned bread dressing mix that you can buy in the bag (like Pepperidge Farm) with chopped up Worthington FriChik® and moisten with vege-chicken broth (either McKays or Bill's Best—add salt if you use Bill's) until moist. Bake at 350°F till hot through and a little brown on top.

No matter how you celebrate, whether traditionally or nontraditionally, with family or alone, the most important part of Thanksgiving is to give thanks. God has blessed us so richly. Each day He showers us with more blessings than we appreciate. Simply being alive for one more year is a precious gift. Thank Him for the miracles in your life, not only on Thanksgiving, but on every day.

CHAPTER SEVEN

Christmas

I love the Christmas season. And I'm talking about the whole season, not just the day itself. When I was young it was all about the presents, but these days I start celebrating Christmas early just because I enjoy it. The Christmas music comes on as soon as the Thanksgiving dishes are done (practically), sometimes even sooner than that if it's been really cold. I make a lot of the Christmas presents we give. If I've been really organized I'll have started these in October and will be nearly done by the time Christmas draws near. Otherwise I'll be working right up until Christmas Eve some years.

There are so many wonderful activities at Christmastime. The Congregational church in town puts on a magnificent production of Handel's *Messiah*. There is usually a performance of *The Nutcracker Suite* at the newly restored Paramount Theatre. Our homeschool group likes to go caroling at a local nursing home and the hospital.

Christmas is a time of warm social events made warmer by the cold temperatures outside. There is popcorn to be popped, cider to be mulled, sledding and snowshoeing to do. Even memories of Christmastime activities are suffused with a rosy glow of coziness not associated with other holidays.

MY TOP TEN CHRISTMAS MUSIC LIST

1) *Miracles*—Kenny G
2) *Christmas at the Almanac Music Hall*—Various
3) *Messiah*—Handel
4) *The Promise*—Michael Card
5) *Happy Holidays, Vol. 28*—Various
6) *Home For Christmas*—Amy Grant
7) *Drummer Boy*—Jars of Clay
8) *It's Christmas Time*—Bing Crosby, Frank Sinatra, and Nat King Cole
9) *Christmas in Manhattan*—Produced by David Huntsinger
10) *The Nutcracker Suite*—Tchaikovsky

One of the activities that leads up to Christmas and keeps our focus on Jesus, rather than the commercial hype that is hard to ignore this time of year is Advent. We usually use a special Advent candle marked with numbers (each night you burn the candle down to the next number) or I make an Advent wreath. The biggest problem with an Advent wreath is that it sheds terribly before Christmas and takes up a lot of room on the table.

I love my friend Sharon Buttrick's Advent idea. "We lead up to Christmas with a special Advent Calendar my sister quilted for us. It has different pictures in each square relating to the nativity and birth of Jesus. Each evening for worship during the month of December we read a special story or Bible verses that go with the picture for that day. Then the children take turns moving a star that goes on the day."

For a couple years we tried to have a 3D Advent calendar, but our house is small and especially with homeschool materials taking up so much kitchen space it was difficult to find a good place to keep it for a whole month. This year I found an Advent calendar that could be put on the fridge. There are also Advent calendars with chocolates inside each door. Now this, I thought, was a great idea.

A word to the wise: If you're going to do the chocolate calendar or a similar type with gifts behind the doors, and you have more than one child, you could be setting yourself up for some additional holiday stress. In our case, disappointment over who got the chocolate each day resulted in us switching to another calendar. The only perk was that Mom got to eat the remaining chocolates.

One tradition we used to have that I've never heard anyone else talk about is the Jesse Tree. On it you hang symbols tracing the genealogy of Christ. My mother used a bare branch stuck in a flowerpot, but you could use a tiny artificial tree, a construction paper tree tacked to a bulletin board, or the lopped off top of your Christmas tree if it's too big.

The symbol I remember the most was a tiny bone. My sister, Faith, and I were fascinated with that little bone. I'm not sure what it was supposed to represent. I thought it represented the jawbone from the Samson story, but that doesn't have anything to do with Christmas, does it? But as a child, it fascinated me and I still remember it. You can hang just about anything that represents something from the life of Christ. You're only limited by your imagination. Here are some other suggestions:

Apple (with 2 bites out of it)—Adam

Toy boat—Noah

Knife—Abraham
Kindling wood—Isaac
Coat of many colors—Joseph
Harp—David
Carpenter's tools; donkey—Joseph (Mary's husband)
Lily—Mary
Cross—Christ
Milk jug—Rebecca
Sheaves of wheat or corn—Ruth
Ladder (toothpicks)—Jacob
Sea shells (try macaroni)—John the Baptist (OK, it's a stretch but use your own imagination!)

You could put these ornaments on the regular, big tree, but by isolating them on their own tree, they won't get lost. Also, it is easy to see the symbols and remember what they stand for. It's a nice, simple reminder of what the season is about.

> *"We used to sing in a choir on Friday evening at a candlelight service. Then we would sing Christmas carols to neighbors. Music was very important in our family."*
> **JUDY COLLINS**

My grandmother remembers her eldest sister instructing the younger ones to stay out of the parlor while she decorated the tree. Consequently, my mom always let me and my three sisters decorate the tree and did we decorate it. Eventually she put our tree (a huge one) up in the basement and had her own small, silver, artificial tree in the living room. We just loved all the loud, gaudy ornaments on our tree, though even as a child I could appreciate how beautiful my mom's tree was with its simple ornaments of white lights and blue balls.

I gave up the decorating of our tree a few years ago. It was about the time Joshua and Rachel were big enough to take over. They just enjoy it so much I can't bear to spoil their fun by telling them what looks better where. The only things I put on the tree are the lights and the glass icicles. I do have my own little tree though. A few years after we were married Rob started giving me a miniature Hallmark ornament each year. I decorate my tree with these tiny ornaments and I love going over each one and remembering which year I received it. It's one of my favorite traditions.

Ginger Harvey lets the kids decorate the tree as well. "On Christmas we have a tradition of inviting the neighborhood kids over. I have the lights on the tree and the kids do the rest. All of the ornaments that are on the tree are handmade each year. I make a new one for each member of the family. I do this so when my daughter gets her own home she will have her own set of love-made ornaments. I now have two grandchildren and they each have their own special ones. After the kids finish the tree we have hot cocoa and cookies, then before they go home they make their own paper ornaments to put on their trees."

Lorene Beaulieu remembers the fun they had decorating the tree. "As a child, we always made Date Loaf Candy. This was my mother's specialty and we would only have it for the Holidays in November and December, which made it special. Also, we would go out and find our own tree in Washington State, cut it, drag it home, and decorate it as a family. Mother would always have hot cocoa or cider available while we decorated. We had an old wind up phonograph that we would play our Christmas records on—it was a happy family time together. Daddy would always make sure he was home early from work so we could get the tree before it was too dark."

Finding the tree in the first place is part of the excitement. We used to go to a Christmas tree farm not far from here and that in itself was a tradition. We always snap a photo next to "our" tree before we cut it down and we take pictures as we haul it home in a sled. A couple years ago we found some nice trees near our home. Now we take a short walk outside to select a tree. Finding just the right tree can take considerable time.

"Each year, Mark, Katie, Jonathan, and I make a big night of the Christmas tree hunt," Gwen Simmons told me. "On the Sunday after Thanksgiving, we go to a Christmas tree farm and spend some time choosing just the right tree. When we have all 'bonded' with a particular tree, we take it home. We decorate it with all of our traditional ornaments, reviewing where we got some of them and what they represent.

"One ornament that we always pay special attention to is a homemade one which says, 'Our second Christmas' on it. It was homemade because in our second year of marriage, we couldn't afford to buy a new one. Nevertheless, we couldn't let the year pass without giving it representation on our tree. After we get our tree decorated, we turn out all the lights and proclaim this 'the best tree ever.' In the cozy tree-lit atmosphere, we then have pizza, root beer floats, and watch *It's a Wonderful Life*."

My pastor, Robert Zegarra, remembers how his parents bought him and his brothers each a special ornament each year. When they were old enough they were allowed to choose their own. One year, young Robert pulled the tree over moving his ornament just one more time. "We always opened gifts Christmas morning and the first person awake could wake everyone else up," he told me. "Each person had to try and guess their present before opening, and we always opened one at a time."

When you get the tree is almost as much a tradition as where and how. Because we burn wood for heat we can't get our Christmas tree too early or it'll dry out and shed all over the house before Christmas. We traditionally put our tree up two Sundays before Christmas. This seems to be just enough time to enjoy the tree before Christmas. Then we take it down about a week or two after.

I love the idea of making or buying ornaments with the intention of giving them to the children when they leave home. I don't have any ornaments from our family tree, though I do have a few from my grandmother's tree that she gave me when she broke up housekeeping.

"When our children were junior-high age we started a tradition of collecting small items from any places/countries we were visiting," says Kathy Phillips. "The items are used as Christmas tree ornaments. We made sure to buy three as we had two children. When the kids grew up and 'flew the nest' we sorted out all the ornaments and they had a good start for their own tree complete with lots of family memories. Some examples are small temple bell-type charms from a family visit to Taiwan, colorful tropical fish earrings from a Christmas diving trip to Palau, llama earrings from Chile, and a Panda key ring from China."

It's amazing what tangible reminders ornaments are of Christmases past. "Each year when we are ready to decorate our Christmas tree, my husband and I have an ornament for each other and one for each of our children," Lisa Whitlow told me. "We have been doing this for all of our eighteen years of marriage. We always put that year's new ornaments at the top of the tree. I have kept a record of all of our ornaments and will give each child their ornaments when they are grown to start their own family traditions with."

The Jay Thomas family starts celebrating Christmas early. "We decorate the tree the day after Thanksgiving. The youngest child directs the decorating. We hang stockings (Mom gets to stuff the stockings) and get out the tea set and the Christmas stories. Every night after worship we sit around by the light of the tree and sip herbal tea as we listen to someone reading Christmas stories."

Christmas stories hold an honored place in our traditions. At our house a recent favorite is *The Best Christmas Pageant Ever* by Barbara Robinson. According to my friend Aileen Andres Sox there's a video as well. "I re-read *The Best Christmas Pageant Ever* and watch the video, too, sometime during the holiday season," Aileen told me. "I often read **all** the Christmas stories I have in my collection at some point.

"I volunteer to read a favorite Christmas story for the Sabbath closest to Christmas during the worship service. It seems more 'family-friendly.' And it helps the pastor if he wishes to travel over the holidays. (He often does his Christmas sermon earlier in the season.) I don't always get the opportunity, but I enjoy it when I do. I've read 'The Christmas Miracle of Jonathan Toomey,' 'The Last Straw,' and the short-story version of 'The Best Christmas Pageant Ever' at various times. All geared toward kids, but enjoyable for audiences of any age. I always keep my eye out for new Christmas stories too."

I'm looking forward to adding some of Aileen's favorites to our "must read" list at Christmastime. And I'm sure the story Penny Wheeler shared with me will be one of our favorites. I hope it will become one of yours as well.

"Starting around Thanksgiving," Penny told me, "on Friday evenings we read Christmas stories aloud. We all have our favorites, and eventually they're all read. We enjoy new ones too. Sometimes we can coax my dad to tell the story of Tucker Webb's Christmas surprise; a man he knew as a boy growing up in Mesquite, Texas."

TUCKER WEBB'S CHRISTMAS SURPRISE
as told to Penny Estes Wheeler by her dad, James Estes

It would be my twelfth Christmas. I'd stretched up tall and gangling. My overalls were too short for my legs; my bony wrists hung below the cuffs of my plaid flannel shirts. My voice played tricks on me. And my hair grew dark and thick; spilling out from under my cap in an unruly way that annoyed my aunt.

I'd lived with my aunt, uncle, and cousins ever since my mother died. I hardly remembered Mamma, so I didn't miss her much. My dad was a building contractor; making houses for others and always sorry that he couldn't give me a home. He worked in Fort Worth. Quite a city. A hundred times bigger than Mesquite, the little farm town where I lived. But, he'd be coming tonight—Christmas Eve. Be in about nine o'clock on the Texas and Pacific, bringing Christmas presents with him.

We didn't have a tree. Almost nobody did. Trees weren't brought in by the thousands from Michigan and Canada like they are these days. Oh, some families might go out and cut down a cedar tree. But mainly they were small and sticky and lopsided.

The church would have one though. They scouted all over the county until they found a good-sized cedar, and then we children made paper chains and the ladies' club strung popcorn to wind around it. There was no electricity and, of course, candles were too dangerous, so the popcorn was about all the decorations it had.

The town was different too. Different, I mean, from the way towns look nowadays around Christmas time. No colored lights twinkled along the street, no plastic Santas winked from store windows, and the dry-goods store didn't have "Silent Night" piped over an intercom to inspire shoppers to buy more.

Not that we didn't have a pretty little town. Built on the Texas flatlands, the buildings rose tall and impressive around the grassy square. In the summer we could pitch horseshoes there. Mesquite was a real nice town as towns went in the early 1920s. But, the stores weren't crowded with Christmas bargains like they are today. A few simple toys like dolls or trains or balls were about all one could find.

Actually, it didn't matter. The farmers and others workers had little money to spend anyway.

Auntie and Uncle Charlie didn't buy presents now that we weren't kids anymore. But in a few hours Dad would be here, suitcases filled with white tissue-wrapped packages for all of us and sacks of fruit and hard candy.

The day dragged by. Feed the cows, milk the cows, eat breakfast, chop the wood, bring in the wood, eat dinner, help Uncle in the barn, help Auntie around the house. At last we finished supper and Uncle Charlie went out to start the old Chevy. I was glad to ride in the car and thankful that we hadn't had rain to make the dirt roads into ribbons of mud. If it had rained, we'd have had to take the buggy or wagon and 30 degrees with a hard wind made it much too cold for that.

My cousin Bud and I climbed in the car next to Uncle Charlie. "Be careful," Auntie called from the warmth of the front room. And then, "Charlie, don't let those ruffians hurt the boys."

I laughed to myself at Auntie mentioning the town ruffians. That's what everybody called them—the group of teenage boys that hung around after dark. I'd seen them leaning against buildings, laughing and joking among themselves, or calling out to people that went by. Sometimes they'd be clustered around Tucker Webb, the town cripple, joshing him in a friendly way. I thought the grown-ups misjudged them. They'd never been mean to me. Sometimes they even spoke and, tongue-tied, I answered, trying to match their lighthearted tone.

I thought about Tucker as we rode along. "Uncle Charlie, was Tucker Webb always like that?" I asked.

"Crippled, you mean?"

"Yes. The way his knees are bent, he can't walk right. And he must be at least a foot shorter than he would be if his legs were straight."

"I guess he was born that way," Uncle told me. "He's never been able to work much, but let me tell you, he's right smart. He reads every book he can get his hands on."

We rounded a corner, the car's headlights sweeping across a barren field. The wind blew dust in little circles in front of us.

"Why'd you ask about Tucker?" Uncle said.

"Oh, I don't know. Just thought of him," I replied. "I was wondering about Christmas and stuff, and thought about him too."

We bounced over a particularly large hole, and then we were on the paved streets of Mesquite. Uncle Charlie drove the car up to the old wooden railroad station, and we all got out and walked inside. Pulling out his large pocket watch, he squinted at it in the bad light. "Train won't be in for at least half an hour," he told us. "Want to have a look around town?"

Of course, we did. Uncle led the way, and we boys did our best to match his long stride. We had passed the hardware store and the post office, and were making our way toward the twin lights that indicated the dry-goods store when we heard a commotion in the street behind us.

"Boys, boys! What are you doing?"

"Come on, fellas. Pick him up."

"Boys, Please ..."

"That's it. One-two-heave-ho."

"It's Christmas Eve, boys. You wouldn't ..."

We turned around and hurried toward the voices.

"See here," Uncle Charlie was saying. But no one paid the slightest attention to his pleas.

The ruffians! What were they doing to poor Tucker Webb?

A big boy stood on each side of the crippled man, lifting him up while he twisted in an attempt to get free.

"Do something, Dad," Bud cried, his eyes reflecting the surprise and fright that I felt. But, Uncle only smiled and shrugged. "Let's wait a minute. I don't think they'll hurt him."

Carried by two strong young men and surrounded by half a dozen more, Tucker Webb was taken down the street and into the dry-goods store. He thrashed around and protested every inch of the way. We, and the others who heard the disturbance, followed. Through the aisles and into the shoe section they went, finally setting Tucker down on a low bench in front of the rectangular boxes of shoes.

"Clerk!" one of them called. "Come here, please. This fella needs some new shoes."

"Bet he has holes in the soles of these," another one said. "Too cold for holes in his soles."

"But I don't have any money. Please, boys, let me go. Clerk!

Don't measure my feet. I don't have a cent."

Bud and I watched open-mouthed as shoes were fitted on Tucker. Then another of the "ruffians" ran up with a couple pairs of heavy socks. "A man can't have new shoes and old socks," he said as he laughed.

Tucker's protests were waved aside amid the boys' talk and laughter. "That man needs a new shirt. Needs two new shirts. And just look at his pants. He has a patch on one knee."

The shirts and pants were wrapped up and placed beside the new shoes and socks. Then a bushy-haired boy picked up Tucker's jacket. "Just look at this," he called out. "How can he wear an old jacket with his nice new pants?"

"He can't wear new shirts with an old jacket," another echoed. "That'd look awful."

"That's right, clerk. Let's see the warmest jacket you have."

"No, no, no. Don't listen to them. I haven't got any money. I can't pay for this," Tucker cried.

Several jackets were brought out and tried on the protesting Mr. Webb.

"Doesn't it fit? Feel good? Do you like brown or would you rather have blue or black?"

Tucker Webb shook his head. "It feels fine. It's beautiful. But I tell you …"

The boys stood in a cluster against the wall, smiling, laughing, poking one another. They were having a wonderful time. "What all do we have now, clerk?" one asked.

"Let me see." He touched each article as he spoke. "Shoes, socks, pants, shirts, jacket. That will come to …"

"Underwear," called out another fellow. "It's freezing outside, and Tucker's wearing last year's long johns."

"Wrap up a pair," a short, pudgy boy called out.

The clerk rummaged around, wrapped the underwear, and placed the package with the rest of the clothes. Taking his pad and pencil, he figured and refigured until he came up with a total.

Tucker shrugged and looked at the wooden floor. "I told you, I'm sorry, but I ..."

"I'll put in three dollars."

"Put me down for two-fifty."

"I'll give you five."

One by one the boys came to the counter and gave the clerk some money. He counted it and looked up. "I'm two dollars short."

In a moment he had it.

Then two boys lifted Tucker to a counter. "Make a speech," they said.

He looked from one to another, his look caressing the face of each of his friends. "Boys, thank you."

He swallowed, gathering pretty words from all the books he'd read. "It is with sincere thankfulness that I express my appreciation for your kind deed. What have I done to deserve such good, kind friends? When the Lord comes, He will remind you that whatever you've done unto the least of men, you did for Him."

He looked at the beaming faces of the boys watching him. "My dear friends, may the God who watches over us all give you a special blessing."

Uncle Charlie dabbed at his eyes and motioned for us to come. We followed him into the night, turning up our collars against the Texas wind.

"Uncle Charlie, did he know what they were doing? I mean, when they grabbed him?" I asked.

"I suspect so," he chuckled. "Fact is, they did it last year and Tucker howled and carried on just like he did tonight."

The train whistle split the icy air with its lonesome call. We stood close together, waiting. The whistle moaned again, closer now, and we could hear the click-clacking of its wheels on the iron rails. The steam made white clouds that seemed to freeze and hang suspended like giant cotton puffs above the train. It shrieked to a stop, and Dad was the first one we saw, his tall frame filling the doorway.

He walked down the steps, a suitcase in each hand and sacks balanced on his arms. I ran to meet him and took the heavy sacks. We made our way to the car, then rode out of the dimly lit town into the black night. Above us the stars hovered thick and low and bright.

It was a good Christmas. Perhaps the best ever.

"The Best Christmas Ever" first appeared in Guide magazine, December 18, 1974.

Lora Hendrickson has found a devotional that their family enjoys at Christmas. Something like this could probably be incorporated into an Advent celebration. "We have a Christmas devotional (*Advent Foretold* by Gary and Wanda Sanseri) we read the month of December. The first half of the month talks about prophecies that foretold the Messiah's birth, and the last half shows the fulfillment of the prophecies. The devotional includes carols that go with each reading and a picture to color. The children enjoy learning to trust prophecy after hearing about its fulfillment."

To order *Advent Foretold* by Gary and Wanda Sanseri, or for more information or a catalog, call 503-654-2300. The book contains "readings for every day in the month of December. Selections for December 1-16 focus on sixteen Old Testament prophecies regarding the coming of the Messiah while those for December 17-31st center on the fulfillment of these prophecies. Professional artwork ideal for children to color. Designed to be used year after year as a family heirloom." Present cost is $14.95.

Also available: "**Advent Calendar Patterns.** Make your own banner displaying 5" by 7" illustrations that match the devotional readings from *Advent Foretold* for each of the 31 days of December. $5.95" and "**Advent Crafts.** Instructions and patterns for making Advent crafts. $5.95."

You can also get in touch with Back Home Industries by writing them at: Back Home Industries, P.O. Box 22495, Milwaukie, OR, 97269-2495.

One of the most exciting aspects of Christmas is the parties. I love Christmas parties and the games that go along with them. By far the most popular Christmas game is the gift swap. I've heard of these five versions. Whichever way you play it, you'll be sure to have a great time. These games are generally hilarious, particularly if played by a group of people who know each other well and aren't shy about "stealing" presents. Check out these versions I discovered and see if one of them isn't right for your next Christmas party.

The first is called the Yankee Gift Swap. This is the one Rob's aunt Sandy traditionally plays at her house. Everyone brings a gift not to exceed $5 in value. All the gifts are placed under the tree. Next each person draws a number from a hat. If there are twenty people the numbers go from 1 to 20. Whoever draws number 1 goes first and chooses a gift from the tree. They unwrap the gift.

Let's say they get a Tupperware bowl filled with Little Debbies. Now number 2 chooses a gift from the tree but before they open it they have to decide will they keep it or swap with number 1 for the bowl and Little Debbies. If they decide to take number 1's gift, number 1 gets whatever they took from the tree and opens that gift right away. Let's say that is a can of cashews. Now number 3 chooses a gift from the tree and has to decide to open it or swap it for the cashews or the bowl.

Because number 1 does not have the opportunity to swap with anyone, at the end, when all the gifts have been opened, number 1 can choose to swap with anyone else in the room. You'll find that some gifts are highly desirable and change hands many times. With this game you never know until the end what you'll really end up with.

A variation of the Yankee Gift Swap is the Chinese Auction. We learned one version at the home of our friends Dr. Joe and Delores Foote of Fort Ann, New York. This was an uproarious game of gift snatching. All the gifts start out under the tree (or in this case on the sleigh table). Everyone writes down ten numbers at random, from 1-50. The "caller" begins to call out numbers, also at random. If your number is called you get up and choose a gift and return to your seat. The gifts are not opened at this point.

Once the gifts under the tree are gone you begin to "snatch" gifts from anyone who has a gift. At times someone will have four or five gifts and someone else have none. When your number is called you roam the room looking for a present that catches your eye and take it back to your seat. Some presents, the biggest ones and those with the most elegant wrapping, become "hot" items, snatched back and forth from one person to another constantly.

When the last number is called, some people will still have several gifts while others have none. Those with no gift now get up and take a gift from someone who has more than one. The hostess will sometimes throw in a gag gift to heighten the fun. The person who receives the gag gift will also get another gift since there will be one left over. When everyone has a gift they are opened one at a time so you can see what was in that box you were trying to get throughout the whole game.

At Delores's party, there was one huge box everyone was after. No sooner was it taken than someone snatched it away. This continued all night. When the gifts were finally settled everyone watched as the coveted package was opened. Inside was a huge, hideous Santa made from yarn. It turned out Santa had a long, illustrious history. In 1993, a patient gave Dr. Joe the Santa, telling him proudly that she had made it for him in thanks for his wonderful care. Dr. Joe accepted it graciously and brought it home to his wife, Delores, who accepted it, shall we say less graciously, declaring it the ugliest thing she'd ever seen.

She wrapped it up beautifully for a gift-exchange party she was having where it was fought over fiercely. Vonnie Edison ended up with it and thought it was cute. Delighted, Delores called all her children that night to tell them she'd gotten rid of the horrible thing. The next morning, she stepped into the shower and screamed. There was Santa.

Today Santa is pretty well traveled. He's been to North Carolina, Kentucky, and Washington State. Once he turned up floating on a raft in Nancy Manzari's pool with a sign saying, "I'm back." He's been left near a car in Kentucky as a going-away present. He even followed Vonnie Edison to a new job and showed up on her desk at work one day, giving her a fright. There's no telling where he'll end up next.

Jerre St. Clair, of Berrien Springs, Michigan has a version of the gift-swapping game I'd like to try sometime. "Now that our children are married with homes of their own, a different tradition has evolved," says Jerre. "We gather at one home for a holiday meal together, each person bringing a $10-$15 wrapped grab-bag gift suitable to his/her age. After the meal we play Bingo. The first person to Bingo chooses a gift and unwraps it for everyone to see. The second person to Bingo can choose either another wrapped gift or take the one already opened.

"The game proceeds until each person has a gift, and then we play several games of 'dirty' bingo where usually there is good-natured rivalry over some 'hot' item. Dirty bingo is where people can take whatever gift they want from anyone else. We usually set the number of dirty bingo games we'll play—say six games. Sometimes a really 'hot' gift—something unusual, valuable, funny or whatever—will be wrested away from another person all six times. This is fun, yet relatively inexpensive."

At some parties the swapping game is "the" entertainment. At other parties, it's only part of the entertainment. Jean Riley sent me a version simply called "The Game," which I learned as a version of the Chinese Auction. "This is a fairly recent 'tradition' that has been established in our family. It is not an especially 'religious' one but it is something that all the family looks forward to nowadays. We all meet at my daughter's house on Christmas Eve for a nice dinner. After dinner everyone in the family is expected to perform in some way—a poem, a vocal solo, story, piano or other musical number, or in some way contribute to the entertainment for the evening.

"But the most fun comes when we play 'The Game.' This is the one where a number of unidentified wrapped gifts equal to the number of participants is placed on the coffee table—everyone gathers around and each person is given a number." In this version, everyone draws a number, as before. Then number 1 chooses a gift from the tree and unwraps it. Let's say it's a mug and herbal tea. Number 2 can either take that gift or choose one from under the tree. The game proceeds in this way. Each person has the opportunity to take something unwrapped previously or choose a new gift from the tree. If someone takes the gift you had, you go to the tree and choose a new one.

"It is sometimes a real challenge," says Jean, "because one particular gift may be something that everyone wants and it keeps getting passed back and forth, adding to the hilarity of the game. And of course the last person to pick may be the final lucky recipient of the desired object. I am sure you have heard of this game, but it has become a family tradition in our family. Sometimes we number eighteen or twenty people for the evening, and it is a lot of fun."

The final version of the swapping game was sent to me by Everett Robinson. "At Christmas time my family of three girls get together at our house along with their kids and exchange presents. We have a 'grab bag game' consisting of gifts worth several dollars wrapped-up and drawn by numbers from the bag. Everyone has a chance then to either 'trade' the gift (unwrapped, of course) to any other one or keep it. Everyone looks forward to this part of our Christmas together."

One thing Christmas usually includes is travel of some sort. Some families must overcome great obstacles of distance to meet at Christmas. "For many years all of our family members have gathered at the folks' place near Yosemite National Park in California," Dick Duerksen told me. "On Christmas day we drive twenty miles into the valley and go ice skating at Curry Village in Yosemite Valley. Hot chocolate, sore knees and ankles, a good snowball fight, and then back home for a great meal. That's Christmas with the extended Duerksen/Crane/Christensen/Zell/Hamrick family."

Our family only has to drive two hours north, but some families have to deal with airports. "Gary and I have a blended family," my friend Rachel Kinne told me. "Often our children would be traveling between parents during the Christmas break. Since airfares are cheaper on Christmas Day and New Year's Day, the kids would usually be flying on those days. With all that traveling between airports and such, a traditional Christmas Dinner really became a challenge. So I opted to have Fondue for Christmas Dinner. We dipped everything we could dip. The specialty dip was a Chocolate Fondue that was adapted from a recipe used at Dante's Down the Hatch Restaurant in Atlanta. We dip every sort of fruit that is dippable as well as marshmallows and angelfood cake. We have a jalapeno cheese dip, hot oil for doing hot dog pieces dipped in batter, and a sweet and sour dip for Morningstar Sausages or Prosage pieces. So whenever we have our kids home for Christmas, we have Fondue for dinner." (Rachel's fondue recipes can be found on pages 74 and 75 of *Adventist Family Traditions*.)

"Our holiday traditions are changing because our children have grown and now have their own traditions and places they must go to—the in-laws," Lorene Beaulieu told me. "However, that said, we usually try to get together someplace on this planet with our family. Because we have to share holidays with the new in-laws, we do Thanksgiving one year and Christmas the next.

"This year, sixteen of us will be going to Hawaii for Christmas. Our daughter lives there and said it was time we chose her home to have our get-together. We will not only have our two sons and their families with our daughter, but we invited our family's favorite aunt and uncle. Along with their daughter and her family, we have set aside two weeks—some can't make the full two weeks, but two Sabbaths together are important.

The menu for our holiday meal is special. "Sometimes we have

whole artichokes as a first course. That is followed by one of our
traditional meals. We may be serving homemade gluten (made from
scratch—not ready-made.) I use a special recipe from my
grandmother after she became an SDA. It has nuts, onions, and
mushrooms mixed in it before the boiling process so it comes out as a
loaf and we use her homemade vegex recipe for seasonings."

LORENE'S HOMEMADE GLUTEN RECIPE

10 lbs. of unbleached flour
5 or more cups of cool water

To make a good doughlike bread knead 300 strokes or about
10-15 minutes (I go by feel). Place in large Tupperware bowl and
cover with water overnight.

Next day—dump out water and wash in new cool water until
you have almost (don't go for completely) clear water. This makes
the gluten. Put through a grinder alternating with walnuts and
onion (about two cups walnuts and two large onions. You can
also add mushrooms. I use about 1½ tablespoons of salt and a
little vegex (my homemade) and mix thoroughly into gluten
mixture. Put all this on a flour sack and tie the ends together
using opposite corners to make the sack.

In a very large kettle, put something in the bottom to keep
the gluten from being directly on the bottom of the kettle. I use a
small metal cake cooling rack—one that is a solid unit. Fill the
kettle with water to cover the gluten, bring to a boil, turn down
to low and let it slowly cook (should be a soft rolling boil) for 2½
hours. Lift out (I use one of those huge meat forks to keep from

being scalded) and place on a large plate. Carefully untie the sack
and place another plate on top so you can invert onto that plate
and let it cool. This is where the family comes in and wants to
start sampling.

Place covered with plastic wrap in fridge until ready to fix for
dinner. I slice it, spread a small amount of vegex on both sides
and fry in olive oil just until lightly brown, and layer in baking
dish as it takes a while to get it all ready. This part can be done
ahead of time and rewarmed just before the meal—using a 350°F
oven for 20-30 minutes.

"We also usually have baked stuffed potatoes topped with butter,
sour cream, and a sprinkle of paprika. We used to use cheese but we
are giving that up for health reasons. Yams are also on the menu along
with Waldorf salad or, for the children, Jell-O fruit salad or frozen
fruit salad. We have carrots or green beans, mixed greens with
mandarin oranges, crumbled goat cheese (some use blue cheese), and
raspberry dressing. And there's usually a vegetable platter—olives,
celery, grape tomatoes, broccoli/cauliflower with special dip. For
dessert we have pumpkin, apple, and pecan pies or sometimes carrot
or specialty cakes. Many times these are saved and served with a hot
drink later in the evening."

Petrine Knight and her family usually travel for Christmas. Once
she and her mom and sister even came up to Vermont for a visit.
"Christmas time is when all of my mom's family goes to New York
and has a blast at my aunt's old house in Brooklyn. All of my cousins
and my sister and I will crowd up in the attic and talk and have fun.
On Christmas day we eat this pumpkin soup stuff (Haitian style) and
my other aunt's homemade chocolate drink—which I think is pretty

eew because it has a thick sediment that settles at the bottom so it's quite grainy. But that's what we eat Christmas morning then we exchange presents."

My sisters and I loved to sing together. We often sang for special music and played various instruments. So, it was only natural that one of our favorite parts of Christmas was going caroling. We had a few carols that we sang from memory, our favorite being "The Twelve Days of Christmas." It was a bit of a challenge to remember the days in the correct order and we always sang it at double speed.

"I remember people offering us money, but never food," Bennie Kritzinger, from South Africa, wrote to tell me of caroling there. "In December we as young people, belonging to a typical small-town church (Long kloof) used to go from farm to farm and sing Christmas carols," Bennie told me. "Sometimes we would be invited inside for a cool drink and 'cookies.' Other people would open the window and thank us. Normally we sang under the bedroom window."

Tim and Lyn Howe and their three boys, Paul (17), Barry (14), and John (11), have a wonderful family outreach program they shared with me. "We have a Christmas neighborhood Lessons and Carols

---

VEGGIE "BEEF" BARLEY SOUP

"I hope others will enjoy this soup as much as our family does. My husband does not ordinarily like vegetables in soup, but he really enjoys this one. It tastes even better on the second day. I serve it whenever my older grandsons, who are all in their 20s now, arrive for a visit since they are so very fond of it. It will also be served on Christmas Eve since we have our big dinner on Christmas day."
—*Anna May Radke Waters.*

2 quarts water
10 tsp. MacKays Chickenlike seasoning
2 med. onions, chopped fine
½ cup finely diced carrots
½ cup finely diced celery
½ cup finely sliced cabbage
½ cup sliced mushrooms
1 small zucchini, sliced thin
1 small yellow squash, sliced thin
⅓ cup barley, rinsed
1 Tbs. dried parsley (or 4 sprigs fresh parsley)
1 Bay leaf
1½ tsp. salt
½ tsp. poultry seasoning

In large saucepan combine all above ingredients, cover, bring to a boil. Reduce heat; simmer 45 minutes until barley is tender.

Then add:
1 can tomato juice
1 can Worthington® Savory Slices and gravy (diced)
¼ tsp. Tabasco sauce

Cook until heated through. Remove Bay leaf. Makes 12 servings.

every year. Eight years ago our children became quite serious about studying strings (much to my surprise!). That year we were wishing to create a meaningful fellowship time with our neighbors.

"Now, we invite all the neighbors that live on our street (it's rural and they are fairly spread apart) and usually we have seventy-five to eighty-five people who come. We have the neighbors read the various lessons and we all sing the carols that correlate with the lesson accompanied by the string group. Interspersed throughout we fit in some 'specials.' We now include some neighbors as musicians.

"At the end we turn out all the lights and Tim reads a talk that he writes new each year about how darkness came to the earth, Christ's mission in spreading the light, and our response to that light in sharing love and help to those around us. He usually shares from his personal experience as a doctor. At the end when he speaks of Jesus coming to earth, bringing light, he lights a candle. Some of the small children take candles and light the candles at the end of each row of seats, till all the candles are lit.

"We sing some more, have prayer, then end. Afterwards we stack the chairs against the walls, serve refreshments, and visit. I never imagined it would grow as it has but now we have two evenings each year. Although it is a big job it has become a wonderful tradition for our family. Our neighborhood is very close and although few of our neighbors attend any church at all this has given us a chance to really get to know more of our neighbors. Some are now very close friends. We've thought of moving it to a large church as eighty-five people is about our house's max, but the house is more personal I believe."

Rick Pearson, who wrote to me from Alaska, remembers a Christmas Eve tradition his mother began. "From the time that I started singing by note as well as by ear, my mother would get the LPs of Handel's *Messiah* out every Christmas Eve. She and I would sing all the choruses and many of the solo parts of that great musical work of praise to our Creator/Redeemer.

"In the years since I have grown old enough to leave the family nest, I have tried to maintain that tradition for myself every Christmas Eve. I join in any available choral group in the local area to participate in raising my voice in the praise and worship of the music. But when there is no such opportunity, I still resort to digging out the recordings and score and going through the oratorio in its entirety by myself. I look forward to the time when we can blend our voices with angels as well as saints in heaven in praise to our Messiah. I'm thankful my mom started such an awesome tradition."

Rick shared with me some original recipes that have gained him a reputation. These would be great to keep on hand in case you get carolers of your own this holiday season.

RICK'S CHOCOLATE-CHIP COOKIES

8 oz. softened cream cheese
1½ cups brown sugar
½ tsp. Mapeline (or other maple flavoring)
2 eggs
½ tsp. baking soda
½ tsp. salt
2¼ cups flour
¼ cup chopped nuts, optional
12 oz. chocolate chips

Cream together cream cheese and brown sugar. Add Mapeline and 2 eggs. Beat until smooth. Mix in baking soda, salt, and flour. Mix in 12 oz. (or more) chocolate chips until chips are evenly mixed throughout batter. Add ¼ cup chopped nuts if desired. Drop by spoonful onto cookie sheet and bake at 350°F for 8 to 10 minutes.

Note: Makes about 4-5 dozen cookies. Because of no butter, cookies do not spread out like the original Toll House cookies do. Dough is stickier also.

RICK'S RAISIN-OATMEAL COOKIES

8 oz. softened cream cheese
1 ½ cups brown sugar
½ tsp. vanilla flavoring
2 eggs
½ tsp. baking soda
½ tsp. salt
2 cups quick rolled oats
1 ½ cups flour
8 oz. raisins (or Craisins)
½ cup chopped nuts (optional)

Cream together cream cheese and brown sugar. Add vanilla flavoring and eggs. Beat until smooth. Mix in baking soda, salt, quick rolled oats, and flour. Mix in raisins (or Craisins), chopped nuts (optional). Drop by spoonful onto cookie sheet and bake at 350°F for 10 to 12 minutes.

If you don't live in a neighborhood that lends itself to caroling you might want to consider caroling at a nursing home like the Hendricksons do. "Last year we sang in the nursing home once a week for all of December!" Lora told me. "We liked it so much we have been singing hymns once a month all year since, inviting friends to join us. Now we are looking forward to singing carols again. We and another family sang to people in our neighborhood last year. It was really fun to make new friends. We had hot drinks and snacks when we were done to warm up.

"We also sang at the nursing home Christmas morning, then had five nonfamily guests for dinner. We all made new friends. This year we invited a different group of friends to go sledding and have lunch. (Sledding is always a winter tradition.) I think it is good to share ourselves with people other than extended family sometimes, especially if they are lonely."

One of the hardest aspects of caroling is getting everyone on the same page, so to speak. Lora Hendrickson solved that problem by making songbooks. "We have special songbooks we made with eighteen common carols in it, printed in yellow with card-stock red covers.

Caroling can also be combined with Ingathering. "I have wonderful memories of Ingathering as a child," Gwen Simmons says. "We would gather at the church, then go in groups walking door to door while someone from our group drove a car along the street with tapes of the King's Heralds singing Christmas carols playing from speakers attached to the car. The people of our town loved the carols and would come outside to listen. Mom would give my three siblings and me a bag of Red Hots to carry in our coat pockets so we could suck on them as we went along. It had nothing to do with Ingathering, but it was fun!

"So when I think of the holiday season, I think of Ingathering as a child. I can still hear the King's Heralds singing 'Hark the Herald,' and I can hear the excited yapping of the Chihuahuas on the other side of the doors. I can feel the warm air seeping from the homes as they opened their doors to greet us. And, yes, I can even still taste the cinnamon on my very red tongue!"

I'd love to go Ingathering in Victorian style like Petrine Knight and her church used to do. What a fun idea! "Christmas Ingathering we used to do with our church. We'd dress up like Victorian people (ladies in hoop skirts and guys in suits and top hats) and we would go door to door singing Christmas carols and Ingather. That was always fun. It was special because I think we were the only ones around to do that kind of thing."

Lora Hendrickson's family goes Ingathering together. "We only go Ingathering/caroling as an intact family. The kids love it, but we only go one night a year. But this year the thought came to mind to take bread to neighbors that we don't know, and sing for them." What a terrific idea!

"For Ingathering this year we are, for one thing, putting cans in stores for collection—like people do here for family members needing assistance sometimes, that have huge medical expenses."

ROY H. STECK

I didn't go Ingathering as a teen because I didn't grow up Adventist, but I can relate to Trudy J. Morgan-Cole's light-hearted memories. "What I recall is Ingathering as a dating ritual—at about ages thirteen to sixteen, when it was still really **cool** to go Ingathering, and hope you would end up in a car with the guy you liked (even if you weren't brave enough to actually be his partner going door to door). I'm amazed to find my youth group kids **still** like this up to about age sixteen—although it's ADRA collecting now. It's amazing to me that there actually is an age at which knocking on doors asking for money is fun. I think the appeal has something to do with the fact that it's done in the dark."

One of the first decorations up in our house is the crèche. I made it years ago and sometimes I think of replacing it, but it's become so much a part of Christmas that another one wouldn't seem the same. We hide the Baby Jesus like my mom used to. We also leave the manger empty, but there is a bag of straw nearby. Each time the children do a good deed they can take one piece of straw and put it in the manger. The idea being that it will be filled by Christmas.

Christmas morning we put Baby Jesus in the manger before we do anything else and we sing Happy Birthday.

"We put the Nativity on the bookcase during worship a week or so before Christmas," Lora Hendrickson told me. "The children love putting each figure in the scene. We read the Christmas story and sing carols. One year the electricity went out as we were getting started, so we turned on our battery lantern and oil lamp. I think using a lantern or lamp will become our tradition now!"

When Karris Neuman's family puts up their Nativity scene they use that time to tell the Christmas story from the Bible. "Every Christmas Eve we have hors d'oeuvres and apple juice," Karris says, "toasting in the blessed time of year. Daddy reads from the Bible the story of Jesus' birth. As he reads my children and I put the Nativity scene up. When Daddy reads that Jesus was born, each year a different child gets their turn of laying Jesus in the manger."

Gifts are a prominent feature of Christmas. Even if you decide to downplay their importance, you still must deal with the cultural expectancy for them. My gift-giving philosophy has changed over the years. At a time when I wanted to give abundantly I never had the money. When I finally had more money the cost of everything had skyrocketed to the point that I could spend more on gifts, but it purchased so much less that it wasn't worth it. Gift certificates became an obvious choice, but to me a gift certificate ranks right up there with cash and if we're all going to go around giving each other cash we might as well forget gift giving and stick to spending time together. Which, when you think about it, isn't so bad, is it?

I could have written Rachel Ashwell's book, *Shabby Chic, the Gift of Giving* because I've been practicing its philosophy for years now. I highly recommend the book if you're serious about giving gifts with meaning that don't cost a fortune. You're invested in the process, which is ongoing, because each gift is created from finds at rummage sales, flea markets, and yard sales throughout the year. These are used singly or paired with new items, but nothing is straight off the shelf, one size fits all. That's what makes them so unique. What it comes down to is putting more of yourself into the gift, versus putting money into the gift.

"Each Christmas, I would take the children out to buy Christmas presents for their siblings and their father. Each year it was with the injunction that they don't tell Daddy what they got him. It was a surprise. And every year when we came home, Daddy would take them one at a time on his lap. The conversation went something like this:
Dad: 'What did you buy today?'
Child: 'It's a secret. I can't tell you.'
Dad: 'Well, if it's a secret, you'd better whisper it in my ear.'
Child: Immediately whispers the secret in his ear."
SANDRA CRUZ

I love this tradition Gwen Simmons shared with me concerning wrapping paper. "I'm not sure how many years ago it started, but there is a particular piece of silver Currier and Ives foil wrapping paper that continues to show up under my parents' Christmas tree each year. For the most part, as kids, we ripped through our Christmas gifts and threw the paper away. But this foil paper was so beautiful it never made the trash. It has been preserved through the years. Now, after my siblings and I are all grown with big kids of our own, it is still used. My sister is the official 'keeper of the foil' and wraps up something in it (though it's quite small now) each year for our mom. Mom opens it ever so carefully in order to preserve the precious piece of tradition. Then as Mom hands the foil wrap back to my sister, we snap photographs of the 'passing of the paper.' There is truly a special feeling of tradition when we see that silver foil wrap appear, and I know that our gift opening would not be the same without it!"

I'm not sure I have the patience to save the wrapping paper, though I always feel a twinge of anxiety when we wad it up. How wonderful to be so responsible with our resources! "When we put up the Christmas decorations, the next step in Christmas preparation was to purchase presents for everyone," Sandra Cruz shared with me. "When we came home from shopping, we took out the box of Christmas wrap and took turns choosing the wraps that we would use that year. On Christmas morning, presents were carefully unwrapped and the paper was carefully folded and put away until the following year. I remember the surprise when my folks actually bought some new paper and we stopped the tradition. None of the new was as beautiful or as cute or as precious as that in the old bag of wrapping paper."

"We divide our family in half for shopping for each other. Last year my husband and the boys set out to find things for the girls (I gave them ideas), and the girls and I looked for presents for the boys. This helps the kids really feel like they are giving, and we can help them find practical or appropriate, simple gifts."
LORA HENDRICKSON

Another important aspect of gift giving is taking the time to appreciate not only the gift, but the giver. "In our family, at

Christmas, we distribute the gifts to the giver," Pastor Edward Allen says. "If the tag on the gift says, 'To Beth from Becky,' Dad takes the gift from under the tree and hands it to Becky. Then Becky gives it to Beth. In that way the giver has the opportunity to make a direct connection with the person they are giving the gift to and the receiver has the chance to personally feel the effect. A special bond is formed between the two. The emphasis is on the giving, on generosity rather than getting. Instead of a chaotic time of trying to see what 'I' got, it has become a special time to savor the giving of appreciation for one another."

Aileen Andres Sox agrees. "We used to open presents on Christmas morning—for Mother and thus for us it heightened the suspense. But she always let us open a couple on Christmas Eve—new pajamas and a game. We also always had to eat breakfast and be dressed before we could open presents on Christmas morning.

"Another thing—and this seems particularly important to me—we took turns opening presents. We'd wait until the person was done and had thanked the gift-giver before going on. People go to a lot of trouble to buy gifts and taking time over them seems so much more thankful and so much less greedy. We never pretended Santa Claus gave gifts either—although we had fun pretending our stockings came from him. Again, kids need to learn that gifts cost money and take a lot of time and effort by *people,* not a mythical elf!"

"When our five children were growing up, our holiday tradition included one week of skiing/winter camp, usually at AuSable in Michigan, which they much preferred versus receiving numerous gifts."
JERRE ST. CLAIR

I think that taking turns opening gifts and listening to that dialogue that always accompanies it is an important part of gift giving. "At Christmas we do the usual—tree, stockings, gifts," Dr. Alison Carleton told me. "My mom really likes the family all home, so we make the trek to California every other year or so (when I am not on holiday call coverage).

"In our family we have always made up a list of things we would like (Mom always says, 'I need your Christmas list!'), and it is sure easier to buy something someone will like when you know what it is! We open one gift on Christmas Eve and then in the morning do the stockings followed by the rest of the gifts. In my folks' home just the kids (that's my generation) and the grandkids get stockings. Also we open our gifts one at a time, each one being watched by the others so we all can see what each one has given and received.

"At my husband's folks', everyone just opens their gifts all at once. But his folks don't really give or expect gifts, so if we aren't there, and we rarely are, we don't do gifts with them, which everyone feels is just fine. Also in my folks' home, and in our home, all the gifts are opened before breakfast. We also enjoy going out for a drive on Christmas Eve to see the lights wherever we are."

Christmas lights are one of my favorite traditions. I've never been someone who likes to drive around just to see the scenery, but at Christmas I make an exception. There's something special about the way they twinkle in the dark.

I've heard of the Twelve Days of Christmas, but I don't know much about it, so I was interested to receive these traditions regarding it. "I used to get **so** tired of the kids asking if they could open 'just one present' every day for the whole month of December," Tammy Cantrell remembers. "So, we have done the Twelve Days of Christmas" starting twelve days before December 25. Everyday (starting December 13) the boys (who are now ages fifteen and ten) get to open one small present that I choose. That has curbed the 'open present itches' they seem to develop when that calendar turns to December! Some of the things that they get to open are: a new book (usually one I got on clearance at a bookstore or from one of those Scholastic book order forms from school), socks, new boxers, school supplies, their favorite snack foods, a coupon for a free video rental at Blockbuster, a Baskin Robbins gift certificate, some 'coupons' that I make up on the computer for '1 free day of Mom making your bed' or '1 free day with NO chores,' etc. In the last four or five years, my husband and I have even joined in, and now the four of us draw each others' names, and then do the 'shopping' for the twelve days. We have a $20 limit—so you have to get creative. It's one of the best parts of Christmas for us!"

Paulette Henderson Straine-Nelson does the Twelve Days of Christmas too. "Every year my children switch off the holiday with their father and staying home. When they are home I do the Twelve Days of Christmas and when they go to their father's, I do Christmas Countdown. This way every year is special. For the Twelve Days of Christmas you start on the 13th of December. At breakfast there is a special box for each child with something in it, a whistle, stickers, a Bible promise, a piece of candy, etc. The same applies to Countdown except I start twelve days before they leave for their father's home."

Lisa Whitlow and her sister Jan have creative ways of staying in touch, not only at Christmas, but throughout the year. "My sister Jan and I have given each other an ornament every year for the past twenty years. We are friends as well as sisters! We also have had a special tradition for the past several years. She lives in Michigan and I am in upstate New York, so we have learned to be creative with our packages.

"When we are together for Christmas, we decide what the plan will be for the new year. We send each other a package on the first of every month. We choose different themes. One year, it was recipes that were seasonal with that month. Another time it was stationery. One time it was bookmarks. One year it was anything with specific flowers for each month. We've done Bible texts, quotes, a particular color of items that were seasonal, a specific theme for each month. One time our theme was friendship. Another year we did a specific 'sense' for each month.

"We also call each other weekly. We alternate who calls. One year, we said that the person who initiated the call told the other something that they appreciated about the other."

Another gift-giving strategy that I'm crazy about is gift recycling. This is when someone gives you a gift that you don't particularly need. Usually you can think of someone who *could* use it. So you "recycle" the gift by regiving it. I used to have a problem with this idea; I just didn't feel comfortable with it. Then I realized that I thought nothing of giving gifts I found at yard sales and *they* were "used."

The Hendricksons recycle gifts. "We have an extended family tradition to give only gifts that are recycled, edible, sentimental, consumable, pictures, or homemade," Lora told me. "This has simplified gift giving considerably. With this motto, we can in clear conscience give away a good book that we have already read, a 100-pound bag of potatoes we got for free, fancy bread we've just learned to make, school supplies, etc.

"At that, our gift giving is limited to the years we are all together (alternate years usually), so cousins and aunts and uncles don't have to mail packages when they are heading the opposite direction for the holidays. It also helps take away the chaos and clutter of gift giving, the unnecessary expectation, the worry and fuss. One year my sister gave me a set of parenting tapes I'd been begging to borrow. I was thrilled!"

Homemade gifts are special gifts. When you make something or offer to do something for someone as a gift you are investing yourself in the gift. "We try to give time gifts," Lora says, "such as coupons for loving services (favorite meals, back rub, etc.) or give a day or two on a project that person (usually the grandparents) needs done.

"I've helped organize photo albums for family members. My husband has helped with the repair needs of his mother's house. Family activities are very important time gifts for children. Children are yearning for connection with their parents, more than they long for more toys. Playing games together, reading books, making sure we do something the children like (besides computer and TV/videos) is a priceless gift."

"Christmas and New Year celebrations can and should be held in behalf of those who are helpless. God is glorified when we give to help those who have large families to support."
ELLEN G. WHITE,
THE ADVENTIST HOME, PAGE 482, PARAGRAPH 3

Christmas is also a great time to teach kids to give to those less fortunate. A woman named Linda wrote to tell me about a wonderful tradition she began with her daughter. "During the Christmas holidays, it can get really hectic. We have tried to teach our daughter that this season is a season for giving, but with such a large family, she seems to get more toys than most of her classmates. (She goes to a small Adventist school.)

"For every gift that she gets, she chooses one of her toys to give to an abuse shelter in our area. At first, she wanted to give away things she didn't really want. Then as the seasons went by and she got older.

She started giving away clothes and toys. She is nine years old now and she starts right after Thanksgiving putting things in boxes to give away."

Ginger Harvey and her husband Earl live on the Hopi Indian Reservation. Their grandson, Rowdy, is living with them. They have a unique tradition to help Rowdy understand the joy of giving. "We have a tradition that we started with our daughter, Angelia. The presents in the stocking are to be shared. Last year Rowdy took about half of his stocking gifts to the kids that were in the hospital, (we do the same for Easter, from his basket he makes one or two baskets to give, for Halloween he keeps eight pieces of candy and gives the rest away). In doing this I am trying to teach that you get a warm feeling inside when you give. It must be working for last week he gave his new gloves to a classmate that did not have any gloves. Angelia, when she was in grade school, would do the same. Once she gave her coat away.

"For Christmas Rowdy uses wrapping paper from his presents, so he has to open them carefully. He chooses the presents that he wants to save the paper from first and opens them. He can tear into the others later. Then he sets the paper aside. After all of his gifts and his stocking are opened he will choose the gifts he wants to share and with whom. Usually it is children in the hospital.

"For Easter he will make baskets out of card stock paper and decorate them by coloring or painting. Then he will divide the grass from his basket and put it into the other baskets and choose what to give. Usually he ends up with just two or three things and gives the rest away. In both cases I do not buy more so he can still have. I always buy what I would for him that way he truly is giving from his things."

THE TREETOP ANGEL
by Pat Moore

The box was marked "To Be Opened December 24." As I looked at the return address, my curiosity grew. Why would my folks send me a Christmas package that I could open the day before Christmas? Gently I gave the box a little shake. It made only a muffled sound. Hmmm . . . that was interesting.

This Christmas season found me far from home with no hope of making a trip east for the holidays. I was a new bride and my husband and I had moved to California to complete his education. I guess I was feeling more than a little homesick. The arrival of the package reminded me of those I'd left behind.

Christmas in our home was always a magical time. The house was filled with the aromas of freshly baked cookies and pies. The delicate red and white "angel bells" sat on the back of the piano. The air was laden with excitement and anticipation. Dad would bring in the Christmas tree and string on all the lights. Then it was our turn to help.

Carefully, we would unwrap the tree ornaments and decide just where they should go on the branches. But the very best part was when Dad would put the angel on the top of the tree. Her delicate porcelain face seemed to glow as she smiled at us. Her silvery wings reflected the light. She had silky white wavy hair with a silver band around her head. Her dress was a pale blue satin and I thought she was the most beautiful angel I'd ever seen. She had graced the top of every Christmas tree I could remember. It just wasn't a Christmas tree without an angel at the top!

December 24 grew closer and with each passing day my

curiosity about the box from home grew. Finally Christmas Eve dawned. Today was the day. I would know what was in that box!

My husband looked on as I carefully cut the tape and unwrapped the box. My eyes filled with tears of wonder as there, nestled in the tissue paper was my old Miss Revlon doll. Only she had been miraculously transformed! She was robed in a dress of white satin and lace. Around her pale curls was a band of gold and she was wearing the most delicate set of crystal clear wings! In place of her legs was a sturdy cardboard cylinder just perfect for placing on the topmost branch of a Christmas tree!

That was twenty-nine years ago. This year, my Christmas tree will again be graced with the presence of a very special Christmas treetop angel. The love and thought that went into her creation make her a treasure beyond measure.

Though holiday traditions are personal, we can all relate to them, and in relating we expand our own possibilities. Bennie Kritzinger, who wrote to me from South Africa, remembers special holiday traditions there. "Every December school holidays we, as a family, went to Plettenberg Bay beach through the Knysna Forest. Then we would stop at a lovely spot to eat lunch and sometimes visit the big tree and watch the elephants. On a Sabbath on the beach while other holidaymakers swam, we as a family would take a long stroll along the beach for several kilometers, exploring nature and collecting beautiful shells. It was always something to look forward to."

The Christmas season is also a time when we are acutely aware of our blessings. Jean Riley recalls one of hers each time she sees the Jolly Juggler. "The year was 1932, the heart of the Great Depression. My father had lost his regular job and in order to support our family he hunted daily for any small jobs available. The local hardware store owner in our small town hired him to come in and sweep the store at the end of the day. It was a day or two before Christmas, and this year was the worst one yet financially. There was no hope of extra money to spend on toys. Having enough money for food and coal was of prime importance.

"My father was very 'handy' and always dependable and the store owner, appreciating that fact, was as generous to him as he could afford to be. He offered to my father a little wind-up clown—its spring had come loose inside and it could no longer be wound up. He assumed it would make a play toy because of its colorful appearance.

"My father brought it home and with great care managed to fix the spring. He placed the little clown on a shelf where we could watch him whirl round and round with his hands in the air, holding a wand that would ring the bell at the end of the stick balanced on his forehead. We called him the 'Jolly Juggler.'

"He became a Christmas tradition in our house, but each year after he performed his delightful little act, my father would carefully rewrap him in blue tissue paper, and place him back in the box to await another year.

"After my father died, my mother continued to bring Jolly Juggler out each Christmas, putting him in the middle of the dining room table where we would carefully wind him up once or twice and watch him do 'his thing.' After my mother died, my sister took him to her home in Oregon. Later she transferred him to my younger brother in California because he had remarried and now had two young boys to enjoy the Juggler.

"His boys grew up and my brother did not care to keep him. He was not yet born at the time we acquired the Juggler, and as a small child did not attach as much sentiment to him as did my sister and I. He readily granted my request to send him back to me in Florida where he again makes his appearance during the Christmas holidays.

"He does not get wound up much; his 'innards' are sixty-eight years old, and any day his spring could snap! So we take very good care of him. His garment is faded, but he still keeps the same smile on his little celluloid face as he bobs back and forth in response to a few turns of the spring. I hope he lives yet a long, long time and continues to help us recall the good memories of those days when life was hard, but much simpler; even though we had little we enjoyed what we had."

Christmas Eve is a special time. Since my paternal grandfather was Italian we always celebrated Christmas with my grandparents on Christmas Eve; it's an Italian tradition. My grandmother made a big meal and Grandpa passed out a special Italian nougat candy. There were piles of presents under the tree, but we couldn't open them until the dishes had been washed and put away.

Now that Grandpa is gone our Christmas Eve tradition has been lost, but not completely. We can't go to the house on Florida Avenue; it's been sold. Grandma no longer makes the big holiday meals. But, Christmas Eve has become a time for us to invite friends or family over to share a meal. And the children are allowed to open the presents I have made for them.

One thing that always made it seem like Christmas Eve to me was the new flannel nightgown my grandmother always gave me. My mother now carries this tradition on, giving the children each a new pair of pajamas. Nothing smells like Christmas Eve like new flannel.

One benefit of opening some presents on Christmas Eve is that it spreads gift opening out a little and makes it less hectic. "We always celebrated opening our gifts on Christmas Eve," my friend Peggy Harris told me. "That carried over to our present family. While my son was still married, his wife grew up celebrating gift opening on Christmas morning so we would meet at our house Christmas Eve and open presents. Then Christmas morning we would go to their house for brunch and presents.

"One Christmas Eve I called my mother after we got home from church and tucked her in with a poem, scripture, and thoughts that I had collected. I had been urgently trying to reach her in the nursing home where she spent her final days in California. Finally that evening I was successful. I had prayer with her and she wondered how I knew that was just what she needed. Early the next morning the nursing home called me to tell me that she had just died. I was so glad then that I had persevered in trying to get through to reach her."

Penny Wheeler recalled one Christmas Eve when she received a wonderful surprise from her daughter. "Several years ago we happily awaited the arrival of our oldest daughter who was teaching in

---

CAROLYN GANK'S PEANUTBUTTER BALLS
Carolyn Gank always makes these Peanutbutter Balls.
Her daughter says that whatever sticks to the peanutbutter ball
she picked up is hers too.

3 cups confectioners' sugar
2 sticks margarine
12 oz. peanut butter
1 tsp. vanilla
Large bag of chocolate chips
3 Tbs. paraffin wax

Soften butter. Mix in peanut butter, confectioner's sugar, and vanilla. (This is best mixed with your hands, as it is too stiff for a spoon. Roll into balls. Melt the chocolate chips and paraffin wax over hot water. Roll balls in chocolate and put on wax paper to set.

Romania," Penny recalls. "She and a Romanian friend were coming home for Christmas. It was snowing that Christmas Eve day, and the trees at the local hardware store were free for the taking. So Gerald brought home a second tree—a beautiful fir with spreading branches. We put it in the living room—just for fun.

"Our daughter Bronwen stayed home when we went to the airport. And when we returned home, we found the tree decorated with lights and baubles. She'd rummaged in the basement and found the decorations. It's one of the highlights of my life—that we came in the house on this unusual for Maryland, snowy Christmas Eve, with our daughter and friend who'd traveled, I don't know, 5,000+ miles, and saw that beautiful second tree.

"Now that we're in Maryland, my father and sister moved up here eventually, too, we do Christmas Eve together. I put the Christmas tablecloth made by my grandmother around forty years ago on the table. Our menu is roughly the same: finger sandwiches, spicy cheese dip, chips, homemade cookies. And we're just there together. Often a long-time friend joins us."

Susan Smalley shared with me her favorite Christmas tradition. "On Christmas Eve we have a candlelight Communion Service complete with foot washing. Before we had children we attended a church that had an evening service like this right before Christmas. We were always traveling back home to spend the holidays with family and never got to participate.

"After we had children, we decided to incorporate the idea into a family tradition. It's an excellent opportunity to draw the focus of Christmas away from all of the commercialism and back to Jesus. It also gives us a chance to share the significance of the service with our children in a very special and personal way.

"The whole family shares in the event. The kids help with preparing the bread, picking out the special crystal to hold the bread and juice, pouring out water and preparing towels for foot washing, reading scripture, and blessing the bread and juice. This has been a tradition that has truly blessed us as a family and we would recommend it to anyone!"

On Christmas Eve Laurie Murphy's family camps out. "We drag out the air mattress, regular mattress, blankets, whatever is needed, and sleep on the floor in the living room on Christmas Eve—we watch movies, read books, tell stories. The kids are allowed to stay up as long as they want/can. The last thing on the TV is the Yule log burning."

Christmas morning is one of the few mornings a year when I can be sure of one thing; I won't be sleeping in. Rosalia Coffen came up with a unique way of catching a few extra winks. "Our boys were allowed to open their stockings first thing Christmas morning— before Mom and Dad got up. This allowed us to sleep in without penalizing them. Besides we always enjoyed hearing their delight with this beginning of Christmas."

Our Christmas morning always starts with a family cuddle as we read the Christmas story from the Bible. I never thought of reading *The Bible Story* books instead. "My parents raised my brothers and me on Uncle Arthur Maxwell's ten-volume masterpiece, *The Bible Story*," Rachel Whitaker told me. "At some point in my childhood we began reading the ten Christmas stories from Volume 7 for family worship each year during the Christmas season. Although my two brothers and I are now in our 20s and could practically recite the stories, we've maintained the custom.

"On Christmas morning, before opening gifts, we always have family worship and read whatever story falls on that day. As we've gotten older, these worships have evolved from a simple reading of the story to in-depth discussion and research (sometimes lasting an hour or more) on everything from whether Mary and Joseph actually had a donkey to how many children Herod killed in Bethlehem. In the process, we've learned a lot about the Christmas story.

"When we finally get around to opening our presents, instead of all of us diving into the pile beneath the tree and tearing open our packages, we take turns choosing one of the gifts we've purchased and giving it to the appropriate family member. We all savor the surprise and delight on the recipient's face and admire the gift before going on to the next person. We've never bought a large number of gifts, but we can still manage to take the rest of Christmas morning opening presents!

"These two traditions have helped make Christmas more meaningful and less materialist for our family."

No matter which version you read, beginning Christmas morning with the story of Christ's birth is a wonderful way to start the day. The Jay Thomas family goes one step further by opening the gift for Jesus before the other presents. "Our Christmas morning is probably a lot like everyone else's. Before opening gifts we eat a special breakfast and read the Christmas story.

"The first present we open is the envelope with our gift to Jesus explained inside. We spend half of our Christmas money on presents for the family and half on something for someone in need. Sometimes it's paying off a natural gas bill so a family can have heat, or buying gifts for children whose parents are having a hard time this year. Whatever it is becomes a family affair, and these are the best parts of Christmas. After the report on the gift for Jesus, we open presents given to each other. We continue reading stories each evening until we take down the tree on January 20 (our papa's birthday). Even our married children still wish to be home at Christmas time because of the warm memories."

Food is an integral part of Christmas traditions. Ronald Dockham sent me a recipe he adapted from Luby's Cafeteria in San

Antonio, Texas. "It is delicious, though a lot of work to prepare. Everyone I have shared the cake with has expressed their approval for it and several have asked for the recipe. It started out as an 'any special occasion dessert,' but turned into a once a year treat for Christmas when the scattered family got back together (more or less). Some of us were in Florida and the others in Michigan so we didn't get together often nor did all of us get together even most Christmas seasons but when we did it was nice to pull all the stops and enjoy a great meal together."

"Robyn Kijura said her mother always made Stollen, which is a German tradition. Also, she made Rice Pudding with almonds. Whoever got an almond would get a gift. The kids didn't particularly like the Rice Pudding, but they would eat it hoping to find an almond so they could have a gift."
LORENE BEAULIEU

While cooking and baking at Christmas time are fun, it can also be fun to let someone wait on you for a change too. "Now, my husband and I don't have children so Christmas tends to be low-key, although we usually get an invitation to Christmas dinner," Aileen Andres Sox says. "There is a wonderful pancake restaurant here in town that opens from 6-2 on Christmas—mostly so that their elderly customers have some place to go for the day. We go there and enjoy a Christmas breakfast together."

"Our Christmas is special simply because we're together."
PENNY ESTES WHEELER

RONALD DOCKHAM'S CHRISTMAS CAKE

Cake:

2¹/₃ cups cake flour	Egg substitute
2 cups granulated sugar	(4 egg equivalent)
2 tsp. baking powder	2 tsp. vanilla
1 tsp. baking soda	2 cups grated carrots
2 tsp. ground cinnamon	1 cup drained crushed
1 tsp. salt	pineapple
1¹/₄ cup salad oil	1 cup chopped pecans

Into mixing bowl, sift dry ingredients then add oil and beat for 2 minutes, scraping sides of bowl while adding the egg substitute and vanilla. Stir in by hand or at low speed and add the finely grated carrots, the pineapple, and the pecans. Pour into 2.9" or 3.7" or 8" greased and floured pans or a 9"x13" loaf pan. Bake in preheated 325°F oven for 45 or 50 minutes. Remove from oven and cool for 15 minutes then turn out on a cake rack.

Icing:

6 oz. cream cheese	1 lb. confectioners' sugar
3 Tbs. cream	³/₄ cup pecans
1¹/₂ tsp. vanilla	¹/₂ cup raisins
¹/₂ tsp. salt	¹/₂ cup coconut

Soften the cream cheese in the cream and vanilla. Beat for 5 to 7 minutes or until light and fluffy. Add salt then confectioners' sugar, one cup at a time, blending well after each addition. Stir in pecans, raisins, and coconut. Ice the cake and enjoy! Preparation time: 45 minutes. Serves: 16. Calories per serving: Who cares?

If you've ever wondered what "figgy pudding" was in the old English song "We Wish You a Merry Christmas," you're about to find out. "Since I was born in England, I make Christmas Puddings each year," Jean Sequeira says. "They are a mixture of nuts, dried fruits, and spices. The aroma fills the kitchen with anticipation of the holiday ahead. (The spices represent the gifts of the wise men to Baby Jesus.)

"I remember my childhood Christmases when Grandfather was still with us. We pulled Christmas Crackers set by each plate, wore the paper crowns (symbolic of the wise men's crowns) which fell out of the crackers as they went off with a bang, then ate our Christmas dinner.

"When dessert time came around, my mother cut the pudding, and guests around the table sorted through their portion eagerly looking for silver coins or ornaments traditionally hidden in the steamed pudding. Delighted cries came from those who found shiny silver, but my grandfather always coughed and spluttered until finally, holding his hand to his mouth, he triumphantly produced a brand-new pound note! I always wondered why he was the one to get the pound. It was quite a few years later before I realized the answer.

"Granddad is long gone but we keep the Christmas Pudding tradition going in my family. Now that my son and his family live in Oregon and I live on the East Coast, I take the ingredients to their home at Thanksgiving when our family gets together. We take time to mix the puddings, each family member taking my mother's wooden spoon, stirring the pudding, and making a personal wish for the coming year. It's a tradition that reaches back into the history of Merry Olde England and helps us remember our ties to that land."

Just thinking about Christmas makes me long for those nippy December days when thoughts turn to family, community, and the birth of a tiny Baby who saved the world. Christmas really is a wonderful holiday, no matter how you celebrate it. I hope you have found lots of new ways to celebrate the most important birthday on earth.

CHRISTMAS PUDDING

1 ½ cups whole-wheat
    bread crumbs
1 cup soymilk
3 organic eggs
½ cup dark brown sugar
½ cup molasses
¼ cup orange juice
1 stick margarine melted
1 cup whole-wheat flour
1 tsp. baking soda
½ tsp. salt

2 tsp. ground cinnamon
1 tsp. ground allspice
½ tsp. nutmeg
1 ½ cup currants
1 ½ cups raisins
1 ½ cups golden raisins
1 cup pitted dates, chopped
1 cup candied cake fruit
½ cup chopped dried figs
½ cup chopped walnuts
½ cup sliced almonds

1. Soak bread crumbs in milk and beat together.
2. Stir in eggs, sugar, molasses, juice, and melted margarine.
3. Sift together dry ingredients, add fruits and nuts.
4. Stir 2 mixtures together in large bowl.
5. Pour into PAM sprayed heatproof bowl.
6. Cover with foil and tie with string.
7. Either stand bowl in a pan with 1" water and bake at 300°F for 2 hours, or pressure cook for ½ hour without pressure and ½ hour under pressure. Cool pan under cold water immediately.
8. Invert pudding onto serving dish.
9. Serve with Bird's English Custard.

CHAPTER EIGHT

Birthdays

I have a confession to make. I hate birthdays. Well, maybe hate is too strong a word. I have a love/hate relationship with them. Part of me is very excited when I have a birthday. That's the part of me that can't wait to find out what lovely surprises are in store that I don't begin to suspect. Another part of me, the excruciatingly shy part, wants to avoid all the attention lavished on the birthday person. This might explain why I usually have such conflicted, disappointing birthdays.

This year it was different. I read an article about a woman who actually celebrated her own life. Whoa—this was a new concept. But, it got me to thinking, why shouldn't we celebrate all God's done for us in the preceding year? We've lived another year, for better or for worse. It's a good time to be thankful for that time and also to give some consideration to what could be improved; a bit like New Year's, but a little more personal.

Above all we should celebrate, and not be shy about it. We're talking about a whole year of life here. And like most circumstances, if you take a proactive stance a birthday can't sneak up behind you and flatten you in a hit-and-run, imprinting you with only the passing marks of another year (otherwise known as wrinkles).

We have several birthday traditions. When I was growing up my mom always served us breakfast in bed. For the occasion we got to choose a box of "sugar cereal." You know the kind; it looks better suited for dessert than breakfast. It was the only time during the year we could do this so it was pretty special.

I also remember one year when I was little my parents gave me pussy willows. In my memory it happened every year, that's how strong an impression it left on me. In reality I think it happened once. Rob and Josh continue this tradition because I like it so much. They scour the back roads for pussy willows and bring me a truck bed full. This year I sat on the porch in the sunshine and made a wreath from them.

The birthday person also gets to choose the shape of their cake. When I was growing up, my mom had this little cake decorating book that showed how to make different animals from layer cakes cut in various ways. On some of the pages she noted which cake we requested and the year. The book is in my possession now and sometimes I use it, but often I just wing it because my kids want something that's not in the book. I've made a hermit crab, a dog, and a mouse (that looked like Josh's pet, Squeak), among other things. It's a veritable zoo.

The Jay Thomas family even does the birthday person's chores. I like that idea. "Birthdays the privileged person gets to choose the menu for the birthday dinner. It's cooked at home, and the birthday person need not help or do dishes or anything. Other family members do all the birthday person's chores.

"Most of our gifts to our children have been in the form of taking them out on a 'date' with Mom or Dad or both. Last year we took

Jon (our fourteen-year-old airplane lover) to the airfield and arranged for him to take us for a flight with an instructor in the co-pilot's seat. Sometimes it's going shopping with Dad or wakeboarding, or whatever."

When it comes time for my birthday my father-in-law is usually the one to sneak 'can't-blow-them-out-no-matter-how-hard-you-try-trick-candles' on my cake. For the kids I like the ones in the shape of the number. One of the things I really like about it is that, if you're like me and several years behind in organizing the scrapbooks, you'll always be able to tell at a glance how old the birthday person was. Dr. Alison Carleton uses a type of birthday candle that sounds like the type I use for Advent. (I recently saw some advertised in the *Lillian Vernon* catalog. They're called the 18-Year Candle. Call 1-800-545-5426 to order.)

"For birthdays we have those candles with ages on them that you burn down through the last age each year," she told me. "My brothers and I all had them and my kids have them—thanks to my Mom. Of course we also always have a birthday cake and gifts and cards. And we measure the kids each year by the kitchen door and mark their height there.

"For our son's birthday we get together with another couple, the age of our parents, since both of our families are out of state, and celebrate. We started this on his first birthday. We had made a cake and everything, but had not invited anyone over. So we loaded up in the car and drove to their place in town and showed up with a party. Now we get together every year."

I think my kids would really love Tammy Cantrell's birthday gift hunt. "For our boys' birthdays, whatever year they're celebrating, I get that many brown paper grocery sacks (if it's their 8th birthday, I get out 8 sacks), and I put a present in each sack. As they've gotten older, the presents sometimes are small, like pencils for school, a new folder for their notebooks, a candy bar, etc. After I put a present in each bag, I hide them all over the house and then we set a timer. (If they are eight years old, they get eight minutes on the timer.) We say, 'GO!' and they have to find all the sacks in order before the timer goes off.

"They bring each one back to the dining-room table and when they get to the last one, they get to open the presents. They have NEVER not finished before the timer goes off. We started this on their 5th birthdays, and our oldest one just turned fifteen. About a month before his birthday he asked me, 'You're still going to do the sack thing aren't you?' "

My friend Sharon Buttrick wrote to tell me of a birthday tradition they have. I love the extra special touches on the birthday tray. "For birthdays, we always serve the birthday person breakfast in bed. We carry it up on a special tray with the best china and a lighted candle. They get to open any cards they've gotten in the mail, saved for this occasion, along with special cards family members have made for them. They also get to be Queen/King for the day and the family members do their chores for them."

Another friend, Rachel Kinne, sent me a wonderful pumpkin bread recipe that her son loves for his birthday. "My son Jonathan has never liked pumpkin pie, but he loves pumpkin bread. My husband, Gary, has a great recipe for pumpkin bread and the kids just love it. Jonathan's birthday is October 31 and so he asks for at least one loaf of pumpkin bread for his birthday every year."

The thing about birthdays is that you don't have to spend a lot to make someone feel special. I love my friend Vikki Montgomery's idea of a birthday week. This is really what birthdays are about. "At a time when we couldn't afford big birthday parties and fancy gifts, we instituted birthday week," Vikki told me. "Starting seven days before the family member's birthday, each day we would do something special yet inexpensive. Some ideas were make a card; make or buy a

GARY'S PUMPKIN BREAD

2½ cups sugar
1 cup salad oil
4 eggs, beaten
1 can pumpkin
3½ cups flour
2 tsp. baking soda
2 tsp. salt

1 tsp. baking powder
1 tsp. ground nutmeg
1 tsp. ground allspice
1 tsp. ground cinnamon
½ tsp. ground cloves
⅔ cup water

Cream sugar and oil together. Add eggs and pumpkin. Mix well. Add dry ingredients alternately with water. Pour into 2 well-greased, floured loaf pans. Bake at 350°F for 90 minutes.

special dessert in a miniature size; eat out at a cheap restaurant (Taco Bell, all-you-can-eat buffet); put fun, cherished, unusual or saved things (stickers, gift cards, for-free coupons, sure-to-be-loved clothing/toys/books/collectibles from consignment/thrift/dollar stores, samples/travel sizes of perfumes, bath gels, lotions, or other gift-with-purchase items) in the birthday person's drawer, seat, plate, lunchbox, desk, locker, bed; allow the birthday person to choose a video from the library or video store; spend extra time at the library or playground; get breakfast in bed; be freed of a detested chore; get one-on-one time with a parent; be feted with songs/prayers/banners/posters, etc. We tried to whip up so much excitement that no one ever felt deprived of a big birthday splash because we had created an ongoing stream of celebration and joy."

Darlene Geiger told me about her traditions for birthdays being a single mother. "This tradition started in our family when my children were very small. I have two girls and it has been a single-parent home since they were two and four years old. Money was usually tight so large parties or lots of gifts were just not in the budget. I began thinking of how I could make it more special and memorable without all the extras that cost so much. I asked, of course, what they would like for a birthday gift and they could choose two, or sometimes three depending on the size and cost, from a list of things they wanted. Then they would choose what their favorite meal was at the time, and of course there was always birthday cake and birthday decorations.

"If they wanted to go to their favorite fast-food restaurant they could bring one or two friends, or if they chose to have their favorite meal at home then they could invite a larger number of friends. As they grew so did their circle of friends, so we began to just do home parties with their favorite meal and they also got to choose whether it was a birthday cake, ice cream, pie, cupcakes, or any other dessert they enjoyed. Through all the years of this tradition there have been changes in choice of gifts. Now it's operas, dinner theatres, musicals, trips to special places, but we still have those special meals prepared with our 'favorite' choices to make us feel 'very special.' The girls are now nineteen and twenty-one, and I pray this tradition will continue with their families because it is a tradition full of very special memories for all of us."

Several families wrote to tell me of a special plate they used to fete the birthday person. My friend Kirsten has such a plate. It's red and reads, "You Are Special Today," around the edges. I know because she used it to serve me a birthday lunch not long ago. Lisa Whitlow's plate even travels with them. "We have a special birthday plate and glass (bought from Syracuse China) that is used for any family member or visitor for the day of their birthday. It even travels to camp or long distances across country for the special birthday person."

"As a PK my folks were not always available for celebrations," Paulette Henderson Straine-Nelson told me. "Therefore I have made a Birth Day an event with my seven children. (four birthed by me, and three stepchildren of my heart). A Birth Day is your very own special day. You are the 'King or Queen of the Castle.' At breakfast you have a special red plate, and you order all day what you want for food and how you want to celebrate in the evening.

"When you wake up, you have a new outfit to wear, whether to church or school. Nothing fancy, just new for you and special. That is the key, you are special and this is an acknowledgment of that fact."

Paulette also shared with me her unusual Birth Day Cake recipe.

HENDERSON BIRTH DAY CAKE

1 box Chocolate Pudding Cake Mix
    (or cake mix and 1 small box of pudding)
1 pint of Haagen Daaz Chocolate Chip Ice Cream
    (instead of oil called for in mix)
2 eggs
1 tsp. vanilla
1 tsp. each: nutmeg, cinnamon

Let ice cream melt for 20 minutes or until somewhat soft. Stir into cake mix and eggs. If too stiff, add a tablespoon of water at a time and mix until creamy. Stir in vanilla, nutmeg, and cinnamon just before pouring into cake pans.

Bake at 350°F for 35 to 45 minutes. This can be made in 2 layers or long rectangle sheet cake.

Brenda Alexander's husband bakes her a real cake every year. "Since before we were married (we celebrated our 32nd anniversary last June), my husband has made a birthday cake for me—not a cake mix, but a true homemade cake of my choice. There was only one year that he did not make a cake, and the reason he didn't has been lost to our memory. Making a cake is his unique way of showing me how much he cares for me, and it makes for a special celebration on every birthday—especially since he usually avoids the kitchen as much as possible any other time of the year!"

Of course, you don't have to stick with cake. Some folks branch out. "For birthdays we were not big on parties," Diane Pearson told me. "Each of our children chose the type of dessert they wanted for their family birthday dinner—pie, cake, ice-cream cake, or cookies. We celebrated as an immediate family, sometimes at home, sometimes in the camper in the woods, sometimes a picnic at the lake."

Birthdays are a good time to reflect and be thankful for the loved ones in your life. My friend Randy Maxwell has a wonderful way to do this. "Whenever someone in our family has a birthday," he told me, "we celebrate by having a special family dinner—usually on the Sabbath following the birthday—and by praying a 'blessing' on them. With our children, my wife and I will lay our hands on the child and pray the priestly blessing given to Aaron and his sons to bless the children of Israel. This is found in Numbers 6:24-26. We insert our child's name right into the prayer and claim the promise in verse 27 that says the Lord will put His name on the children and will bless them. We always feel very close to our children when we do this, and they, in turn, respond with hugs and smiles. They feel loved, special, and set apart."

Judith Newton sent me a sweet tradition her daughter Jacqueline Giles began with her children. "Jacqueline has one of the most unusual yet touching ways of sharing 'birthday' with her children. She has three children: two girls and one boy. The girls are sixteen and thirteen years old; the boy is eleven. Ever since they were little toddlers and old enough to understand, Jacqueline has made their birthdays very, very special to them.

"Each year right before their birthday she tells them all about their birth. She shares with them how excited she was that she was going to have them, how special she knew they would be, how much she prayed for them. Then the day of their birthday and right before the 'hour' in which they were born, she starts sharing her 'birthing experience' with them. She shares with them how she is now having labor pains and she can't wait until they are born. At the hour that each one was born she hugs them and tells them how glad she is that they were born! It's incredible how much this has touched the lives of her children.

"I've watched through the years as each child has made a point to go through this with their mother. What is neat is that two of them were born in the late evening. The older girl is sixteen now and my daughter thought perhaps she was too old to really enjoy this, so Jacqueline didn't wake her up. When her daughter woke up and realized that Jacqueline had not woke her she was really upset. 'You didn't wake me up to be born,' was her lament.

"It's a simple thing, but so very special to each child. Each one relives the excitement of their birth and how 'special' they are to their mom. This has only increased their spiritual walk as Jacqueline always reminds them that God gives life."

Most of the time, in my extended family, we don't get to see the birthday person on their actual birthday. Even if we have celebrated ahead of time, it's a tradition for all family members to call the birthday person and sing "Happy Birthday" over the phone. It's a nice way to feel remembered on your special day.

"For birthdays our tradition is to call the person first thing in the morning and sing Happy Birthday to them over the phone on a speaker phone if they are away from home," Linda Downs told me. "If they are home we sing to them while they are in bed and have a card and present waiting at the breakfast table so they can feel special all day."

"Growing up Adventist from the time I was four, my parents started the tradition that every time one of us three children had a birthday, they would give a thank offering to the Lord, the amount being the same as our age. Even now at the age of thirty, they still keep it up."
HONEY FRAPPIER

And where would birthdays be without cameras? We use standard 35 mms, but I have the most fun with my Yashica, which is a large format camera. It's one of those old-fashioned ones that you look down into. People never suspect you are taking their picture because you aren't looking at them so you get some great candid shots.

"We shoot a lot of pictures," Ernie Medina, Jr. told me. "And we also do a lot of video, especially since we had our daughter Summer Alyssa three years ago. Besides shooting a lot of film of her, we have reserved one tape where we dub all her b-days on it from year to year. Then when you watch 'Summer's B-days' tapes, you can see her growing and changing from year to year. It's pretty dramatic when you have it all back to back and a great idea before you lose those birthdays amid the boxes of home videos."

I remember (and I'm sure this dates me) when we used to sit in the little alcove off the kitchen at my grandmother's house and watch all the old home movies. We'd set up the screen and Grandpa would get the projector going. It was great fun to see what we were like as children. How neat to make it a birthday event like Douglas Tilstra's family does.

"We just finished celebrating our son's 14th birthday tonight and continued a tradition we started when our kids (now seventeen, fourteen, and eleven) were just toddlers. After birthday supper (their menu choice, of course) and presents we do a slide show that chronicles the birthday child's life from birth to present. Tonight it was Stephen's turn. We relived the day he was born (Thanksgiving Day 1986) and all the events surrounding his birth.

"We saw mud pies, forts, and water fights. We remembered his first bike and first bike crash. We were reminded again of his love for animals and all the special ones he has loved and lost. We laughed and remembered and affirmed. Then we surrounded Stephen and prayed for him—thanking God and asking a blessing on him. Often we take turns affirming and blessing the birthday person in the middle before we pray—but tonight it was late and we just prayed.

"When I put Stephen to bed he hugged me and said, 'It's been such a great birthday. I love you, Dad.' Later that night, my wife, Lorraine, commented, 'Did you notice John and Elisabeth's prayers for Stephen? Their prayers went way beyond even what you and I thought to pray for Stephen. They're carrying the momentum of this tradition on their own now!' "

"For the children's birthdays, instead of parties, we usually will buy a family membership to the zoo or museum—something we wouldn't be able to afford if we sprung for a big party."
LAURIE MURPHY

Lora Hendrickson and her family have many inventive birthday traditions. "We have a birthday in December. Last year the theme was 'Tropical Snowman.' Her cake was a snow lady dressed in Hawaiian style clothes; very simple and healthful. We ate tropical fruit and nuts, and the grandparents really got into it. Because they had already furnished her with a lavish sugar-filled birthday party and lots of presents, this birthday party was 'No Gifts' and we had puppet shows and piano recitals instead. Fun! We gave our daughter her presents from us earlier in the day. We are working on de-emphasizing gift receiving for birthdays and Christmas.

"Also, a birthday tradition we started with our kids at age three is that Daddy takes the birthday person out for breakfast. If he can't that very day because of work, it is some time that week. This year our ten-year-old had the option of going on an overnight backpack trip with just Daddy or the breakfast; now that is the new 'rite of passage' and the other kids are looking forward to going backpacking with Dad. (It rained on them, but they had a great time and eagerly showed us later exactly where they put their tent, etc.)

"The mother is in charge of the father's birthday, and we always try to make a surprise. This year my husband went on a treasure hunt! He had to climb the apple tree, swing on the swing, start the pick-up, etc. and at each stop also read a scripture that revealed a TRUE treasure (Jesus, children, family, etc). It was a Bible study en route! At the end, he had to find his present we had buried somewhere, which he did valiantly.

"The father is in charge of the mother's birthday. He's made a special effort to out-do himself and the previous year's homemade cake. (This is a man that doesn't usually spend much time in food preparation.) This year's cake looked so good, I thought he bought it! They were having a particularly difficult time this year, because I was home and they had planned a surprise party with friends. How were they to finish their plans?

"They snuck around behind my back, frosting the cake in a room they hoped I'd not go in to. A few things made me suspicious, so I made a special effort to clean the house well. I was glad later because we had a houseful of friends! My husband told me later, 'You just have to be ready all the time!' "

And Kendra Hayes wrote me about a tradition in her family. I'd never heard of golden birthdays before, but I do remember that the year I turned ten on the 10th felt very special. "We have the tradition of golden birthdays," Kendra told me. "You get a gold or silver ring with your birthstone in the middle and your name engraved on the ring. Your golden birthday is when the day and year match. If you were born on August 20th your golden birthday would be when you turned twenty on the 20th."

Kendra also shared with me some recipes from her Native American heritage.

Birthdays are a celebration of life and accomplishment as well as an opportunity to appreciate the passing of another year. I've been inspired by the ways you celebrate birthdays. I hope you have too. We have a lot to celebrate.

NAVAJO FRY BREAD

2 cups white flour
1 tsp. salt
2 1/2 tsp. baking powder
2 tsp. dry milk

2 tsp. shortening
3/4 cup of warm water
Shortening for frying

Mix the dry ingredients in the bowl. Then mix in the shortening with your fingertips. Add the water and work into a soft dough. Cover and let rise for 15 minutes. Roll the dough into a long log. Cut off small pieces of dough about the size of a golf ball. Roll each ball between two pieces of waxed paper to flatten.

Fry in smoking-hot shortening in an electric frying pan. Fry till about golden brown all the way around. Then take out and place on paper towel. Once cooled, serve with salt, peanut butter, or honey.

SWEET POTATO PIE
pref. = *preference*

2 unbaked 9-inch deep-dish pie shells (about a 4-cup volume)
1½ cups granulated sugar
1 tsp. salt
2 tsp. ground cinnamon
1 tsp. ground ginger
½ tsp. ground cloves
4 eggs
3 cups evaporated milk (two 12 oz. cans) pref. Carnation®
3½ cups (29 oz. can) candied yams or plain yams (your pref.)

Combine sugar, salt, cinnamon, ginger, and cloves in medium bowl. Beat eggs lightly in large bowl. Stir in pumpkin and sugar-spice mixture into large bowl with eggs. Gradually stir in evaporated milk. Pour into pie shells.

Bake in preheated 425°F oven for 15 minutes. Reduce temperature to 350°F and bake for 40-50 minutes or until knife inserted near center comes out clean. Cool on wire rack for 2 hours. Serve immediately or stick in fridge.

CHAPTER NINE

Anniversaries

There's something about an anniversary that is so satisfactory. The steadily climbing number of years is like a monument to love and determination. Marriage isn't easy. But, it is worthwhile, which most easy things are not. Big anniversary numbers usually come at a cost, but their reward is with them. By growing together and learning to give and receive love, we become better people and a better couple. And that is its own reward.

I don't know many people who have been married more than ten years who haven't gone through some kind of marital problems of the sink or swim variety. It is a testament to their tenacity and commitment to each other that they are still swimming, many of them in Olympic-sized pools. These people are an inspiration to me. Marriage is one of the most worthwhile covenants we will ever make and one of the most rewarding. We should celebrate it accordingly.

The Jay Thomas family celebrates anniversaries in style.

"Anniversaries are great. Our extended family lives nearby. Whenever someone has an anniversary, the others take care of the kids, dogs, house, or whatever so the anniversary couple can either get away for an evening or a day or two, or just stay home and be alone together, as they see fit."

Because our anniversary falls on Valentine's Day, as I said, our own celebration gets caught up in the celebration of Valentine's Day. Sometimes we even find cards that combine the Happy Anniversary/ Happy Valentine's Day sentiments. Robin Froelich and her husband have taken that one step further. "My husband and I are both very frugal. I have saved most of the cards he gave me when we were dating in a large scrapbook. So at anniversary time, he or I choose one of the cards from the book and 'give' it to each other 'again.' It may sound very cheap, but we love it. We think back and reflect and laugh together!"

Boxes of love notes are great things. Rob and I each have one filled with letters we wrote each other when he was in college and I had just finished nursing school in Vermont. It is fun to go back and read them. It's like opening a time capsule. Joel and Victoria Ingram didn't stop writing love notes when they got married. They are continuing to build their "time capsule."

"Victoria and I have a box in which we put notes about things that happen during the year," Joel told me. "It can be something funny, something romantic, something unique, etc. Then on our wedding anniversary, we pull out the camcorder and tape ourselves reading them and just reflecting on the past year. We also have a rule; we only watch the tape every three years. When we have our 25th or 30th anniversary, I guess it will be interesting to see how we've changed together— as a couple/physically/spiritually, etc."

Renewing vows is another way to make an anniversary special. What an awesome way to recommit yourselves. And what a great excuse for a celebration! Why should the young marrieds have all the fun? You don't even have to be approaching a special anniversary. Rob and I renewed our vows at a Caring For Marriage retreat several years ago, but I'd love to do it again with all the trimmings. Maybe I got stardust in my eyes at my youngest sister Joy's recent wedding. I don't know. But, one thing I am sure of, commitment should be celebrated and so should the kind of love that upholds it.

CHAPTER TEN

Miscellaneous

This chapter is a hodge-podge of traditions not covered anywhere else. Personally, I like finding little holidays, tucked away, maybe forgotten by most. One of these, Bastille Day, which falls on July 14, has become one of our favorite holidays. It all started when our group of friends decided to schedule a Game Night on Bastille Day. The husband of the couple whose house we were going to be at is a chef and he was going to make a French entrée. The rest of us were going to bring French side dishes and desserts. I was really looking forward to it.

Then someone cancelled, but I had really been looking forward to having this French dinner. I'd been to a Bastille Day celebration once, with members of my French conversation group, and it was one of the most memorable events I've ever attended. So, we decided to celebrate anyway. I pulled out my Vegetarian Bistro cookbook and got to work. We ended up having a wonderful meal and great conversation with friends. It's a tradition we intend to keep up.

BASTILLE DAY WHITE BEANS
WITH GARLIC AND OLIVES

1 clove garlic
Pinch of salt
2 Tbs. olive oil
¼ cup pitted Kalamata olives, chopped
1 tsp. drained capers
Pinch of Herbes de Provence
2 cups drained cannelloni beans
Squeeze of lemon juice

Crush garlic and salt in a mortar or food processor. Add olive oil, olives, and capers. Stir to make a thick, lumpy sauce. Season with Herbes de Provence. Combine with beans. Add lemon juice. Serve at room temperature.

I remember watching the parade as it passed by our house on the Fourth of July when I was a kid. I've never been all that crazy about parades, to tell the truth. But, it seems only fitting to do something patriotic on July Fourth. Last year we had a picnic for our homeschool friends and watched the fireworks from our front lawn, which is one of the best places in town to see them. This year I'd like to try going to a nearby farm where I hear they have activities and people dress up and give patriotic speeches.

"For Fourth of July we get together with an older couple in our church," Dr. Alison Carleton told me. "Since our folks live out of state and so do their kids, we eat a meal at our farm and do a few small fireworks and then go into town to watch the big fireworks."

I've heard of some obscure holidays, but a Blue Moon wasn't one of them until now. I like it though. Rick Pearson sent me recipes for Date Nut Cake and Corn Casserole that he has for "birthdays, Thanksgiving, or even once in a blue moon.

"The date-nut recipe was one that my grandmother, Cleora Jones, used to make for special occasions," he told me. "She has been gone for nine years now. The Corn Casserole recipe is still enjoyed every time that I take it to potluck."

Friends of ours, Michael and Kirsten Spafford, always make a banner and cards for the veterans on Veterans Day. They make sure

---

DATE NUT CAKE
Note: You'll get the best results if you mix by hand but don't overmix.

1 cup chopped dates
1 cup boiling water
1½ tsp. baking soda
1 cup mayonnaise
1 cup sugar
2 cups flour
2 tsp. vanilla
½ cup chopped nuts

Mix together dates, water, and baking soda. Let stand until cool. Add mayonnaise and sugar; mix together by hand. Add flour; mix well. Add vanilla and nuts. Pour into greased and floured 9"x13" cake pan. Bake at 350°F for 35-40 minutes or until toothpick comes out clean. Let cool then frost if desired. My personal favorite frosting with this cake is a maple flavored, cream cheese frosting—1 pkg. cream cheese + powdered sugar + maple flavoring.

CORN CASSEROLE

17 oz. can cream style corn
17 oz. can whole kernel corn
½ cup melted butter
2 eggs (beaten)
⅔ cup yellow cornmeal
1 tsp. salt
1 cup sour cream
1 cup cheddar cheese (shredded)
⅓ cup green pepper (chopped)

Mix together all ingredients. Bake 1 hour at 350°F.

the kids in our homeschool group are included as well. They present the banner at a dinner held for the veterans. So far we haven't been able to go because we don't get back from church early enough, but someday I'd like to be part of that presentation. I often think about how indebted we are to our veterans.

Paulette Straine-Nelson was kind enough to share her tradition for Veterans Day with me. "Since my husband is a Vietnam Veteran, we celebrate Veterans Day. I usually come home early and the kids have already lined the walkway with small flags. We make a special meal of all his favorites and end it with either Strawberry Blueberry Shortcake, or Raspberry Torte with blueberry sauce, something red, white, and blue. Sometimes the kids dress up in fatigues, or their Pathfinders uniforms, combat hard-hats, etc. We say the Pledge of Allegiance after the blessing of the food."

Some of the most special traditions are the "Just Because" traditions. Paulette also shared with me some of the meaningful little touches she uses to let those around her know how much she cares. "My parents were not into children, so my brother and I didn't always feel that our birthdays and holidays were any big deal. When I had children, I vowed to make every holiday and birthday a 'high' in the journey of life. So for every holiday, in their lunches, I put special love reminders. It might be a love note for Valentine's with heart candy, or for Easter an egg candy or bunny miniatures, May Day flower notes, for June a countdown to the end of school. For the beginning of school at the end of the first week we have pizza and root beer floats. In October I start with jokes and pumpkin themes, but I'm not much into scary stuff. Before Thanksgiving vacation I usually take them to see a movie or we rent a movie with popcorn and all the trimmings because we need a break before the onslaught of family and making the big feast.

"In the love notes you tuck into lunches, it's very important to be short, sweet, and to the point because they will be balling it up and throwing it in the trash before anyone can see that mushy stuff. But trust me, they love it. Try to pick a specific trait or act that you appreciate such as, 'Thanks for taking out the trash! I LOVE YOU! Mom & Dad,' or 'You really lift my day! Love, Mom.' Don't forget your spouse! They love to be surprised just as much. Once I ordered pizza for my husband and had it delivered to his office as a surprise. Wow, did he feel loved and cared for. My husband has surprised me with a huge bouquet of 'grocery store' flowers and a big note tucked inside saying, I LOVE YOU!!! The 'love cup' was full and running over."

If I had to give an award for the most unusual tradition I received this would have to be it. I am on a mission to find a microwaveable muffin tin just so I can try this. I'm sure my kids will love it. It came to me from Louise Benitz and apparently might have been lost in the mists of time if it hadn't been for her sister.

"My sister reminded me about a little 'family tradition' that we had when my children were young and still at home," Louise told me. "I really didn't think of it as a 'family tradition' until my daughter asked me for my recipe for our Friday Night Egg Baskets recently as she is starting her own family. This is not a holiday tradition but just a Friday night Sabbath supper tradition. It is fairly simple and easy to make for supper and we usually had candlelight along with it and some kind of fruit and hot chocolate."

Afternoon tea is another one of those little traditions that I like to celebrate regularly. To me it seems like a big deal because I haven't always done it. Actually I have two ways of having tea. Sometimes I'll

---

FRIDAY NIGHT EGG BASKETS
(Microwaved—you need a microwaveable muffin pan.)

1 1/2 cups cornflakes
1/4 cup melted butter or margarine
3/4 cup grated cheddar cheese
6 eggs

Crush the cornflakes in the melted butter/margarine. Spray the muffin openings with vegetable spray and then line the openings with this mixture making a nestlike hole in the center of each large enough for an egg. Break an egg into each nest of cornflakes. Use a fork tine to just break the egg membrane at the top (keeps the egg from exploding while cooking in the microwave). Sprinkle salt and the grated cheddar cheese over each egg. Microwave on high for about 4 minutes—turning the pan often.

simply prepare a cup and sit down with a good book. Now, the important part here is to use the "good stuff." It doesn't count if you make the tea in a mug, no matter what a favorite it is.

You have to use teacups, preferably in some pretty English chintz pattern or something equally dainty and pretty. And we're not just talking about the cup part here. You've got to use the saucers as well. It's a mental thing, I admit. Rather like insisting on a real tree at Christmas or wooden cross-country skies instead of fiberglass. What it actually does is convey to you that *you* are important. Most people will go all out to entertain friends, but seldom extend themselves the same little courtesies.

Basically tea and a nice teacup and saucer are the baseline requirements for a tea. If you want to add on you can serve the tea on a tea tray with a pretty cloth, napkin, small vase of flowers, even cookies or cake, if you want to be on the fancy side. Of course, to really qualify for fancy you must make tiny little tea sandwiches and have a selection of cakes and cookies as well as something to slather on the top like lemon curd or clotted cream. The whole point, however, at least for me, being to take a break, I don't usually put much extra effort into the affair.

The other kind of "tea" I have isn't really a tea at all, but it's similar so I sometimes refer to it as a lemonade tea. I'll make up a pitcher of lemonade and put it on the tea tray with some glasses (clear glass) and cookies. Then the kids and I will carry it out and sit in the shade and read a good book aloud. This is one of our favorite summer traditions.

As you can see, traditions can be celebrated for any reason, at any time. They don't even have to mean anything to anyone else as long as they are important to us. They are part of what makes our families unique and create the kinds of bonds that hold us together during good times as well as bad times.

I hope you've enjoyed this trip through the holidays with me. And I'd like to thank everyone who contributed special holiday traditions. You've added sparkle and meaning to our own celebrations. This scrapbook full of holiday memories is a testament to your creativity and your dedication to God and family. God bless each of you during the holiday seasons and throughout the year.

Recipe Index

If you enjoyed this book, you'll enjoy these as well:

Adventist Family Traditions
Céleste perrino Walker. A wonderful collection of family traditions harvested from Adventist members around the world. Customize them for your family, and use them to build a special history that will strengthen your bonds to family, church, and God.
0-8163-1876-X. Paperback.
US$9.99, Can$15.99.

Making Sabbath Special
Céleste perrino Walker. The art and joy of Sabbath keeping is becoming lost. Here's a book designed to provide simple traditions to make the day a delight.
0-8163-1706-2. Paperback.
US$9.99, Can$15.99.

Family Sabbath Traditions
John and Millie Youngberg. An inspirational and practical guide to help your family fill the Sabbath hours with joy. Two cover options!
Caucasian family: 0-8163-1848-4. Paperback.
African-American family: 0-8163-1854-9. Paperback
US$9.99, Can$15.99.

Joyous Christmas Traditions
Evelyn Glass. A nostalgic and fun guide to making the holidays memorable and fun for everyone. Includes favorite holiday recipes, seasonal stories and more.
0-8163-1797-6. Paperback
US$4.97, Can$7.97.

Order from your ABC by calling **1-800-765-6955**, or get online and shop our virtual store at **www.adventistbookcenter.com**.
- •Read a chapter from your favorite book
- •Order online
- •Sign up for email notices on new products

Prices subject to change without notice.